Redemption

The Next Phase…

by

Bert Robinson

Foreword by Frank Nichols

Copyright © Bert Robinson
Foreword by Frank Nichols

All rights reserved. No part of this publication may be reproduced, distributed, or transmitted in any form or by any means, including photocopying, recording, or other electronic or mechanical methods, without the prior written permission of the publisher, except in the case of brief quotations embodied in critical reviews and certain other noncommercial uses permitted by copyright law.

ISBN-978-1-951300-36-4

Liberation's Publishing LLC
West Point - Mississippi

Redemption
The Next Phase...

Bert Robinson

Foreword

This is one the few autobiographies that accurately portrays a juvenile delinquent lost to the streets. In his new book release Redemption, Bert Robinson shares some his most intimate life experiences; from being a juvenile delinquent, selling drugs, sexual abuse, to homelessness. Throughout the early years of his life, Bert earned mad street creds largely because of his gift of gab. Despite being young, his name carried a lot of weight in the hustle game. He persevered despite being sexual abused, addicted to selling drugs, and later in life addicted to sex. With life spinning out of control, Bert still felt the need to give back as a means of Redemption.

After being incarcerated, while in jail he was able to reflect on the lessons taught to him by his parents. His mother Mildred was one of the handfuls of successful black business owners in Oktibbeha County. Ironically, her business was located across the street from the Oktibbeha County Jail of which the likes of Johnny Cash was held. His father who was Bert Robinson, Sr., was one of the wealthiest African Americans in the county. He owned one of the largest black funeral homes in the area. Bert Sr. was also a well- documented civil rights activist during the turbulent 60's in Mississippi.

It is rare to see and read such transparency shared by a person whose morals derived from the codes of the streets. After reading this personal testimony, it required me to take a deeper look at the man in the mirror and ask myself, am I giving to a greater good as Bert has in this revealing autobiography. This well written personal assessment of oneself will leave you questioning your existence. This is a must read for those seeking to redeem themselves…

R. Frank Nichols
 Retired Chief of Police

Redemption

"I come to you hungry and tired, you give food and let me sleep

I come to you weak, you give strength and that's deep

You called me a sheep, and lead me to green pastures

Only asking that I keep the focus, in between the chapters

You give me the word, and only ask I interpret

And give me the eyes, that I can recognize the serpent

You know I ain't perfect, but you'd like me to try

Unlike the devil who just wants me to lie, till I die

Lord why is it that, I go through so much pain

All I saw was black, and all I felt was rain

I come to you because it's, you who knows

You showed me that everything is black, because my eyes were closed

You gave me the light, and let me bask in your glory

So, it was only right, that when you asked for this story

I put together, to do our people some good

Our people being brothers and sisters in the world

Plenty of times you sent help my way, but I hid

And I remember once you held me close, but I slid

There was something that, I just had to see

That you wanted me to see, so I can be what you wanted me to be

And I think I've seen it, cause I don't feel the same

Matter of fact I know I have seen it, I can feel the change

And it's strange, almost got me beating down your door

But I've never known love, like this before

Redemption: The Next Phase…

It's a wonderful feeling, to get away from the pain
And up under the ceiling, I get away from the rain
And the strain that I feel when I'm here, is gone
I know real so I wipe away the tears, with a song
And I almost lost faith, when you when you took my man, Bert Robinson
And I fear that what I'm saying, won't be heard until I'm gone
But it's all good, 'cause I really didn't expect to live long
So, if it takes for me to suffer, for my kids to see the light
Give me pain till I die, but please lord treat them right"
DMX

Introduction

Redemption is the act of saving or being saved from sin, error, or evil.

When you look back over your life and think of the countless times redemption was needed, the smallest and simplest events can become a part of your personal redemption story. I need you to think for a moment. Just for a moment. I am asking you to stop and put the book down. Now that the book is down, I need you to open your heart, mind, body, and soul. I know you see it; I know you can feel it. I know you can smell it, and your heart jumping with excitement as you think on your redemption story.

Well, I know mine is beating faster and faster with the excitement of my redemption journey.

Ask yourself, "How many times did I have to redeem myself?" Throughout this book, I will walk you through my journey of Redemption. This journey took me to many dark places in my life, relationships, parenthood, communities, and manhood.

Also, make sure while reading this book, as I cover a different section of my life that you take a moment and reflect on your personal experiences. I would like you to relate to my stories. They may be or may not be your own experience. Either or, this book will help you or someone else. I cannot say I will be in chapter one or chapter three. I just know this book will grab you and make you think about certain things.

So, when you did ask yourself, how can I redeem myself from a past lifestyle, career, as a person, relationship, and a parent? I want you to know it is never too late for your redemption story.

It could be that degree you wanted to obtain, go get it, weight lost, start on it, that business venture in your head or you wrote down, go create it, you messed up a relationship with your kids, mate, or family member, go reclaim it. And, if your evil deeds out weight your good, please, I challenge you to take your life back.

Your redemption story is a story someone who believes in you need to hear to motivate them. Your testimony might be the story to save a generation of people. People around your household, community, or it is a tremendous possible a person, you have no idea is watching you need it.

That person is just waiting for you to speak about your personal life story and give them the encouragement to change their own life. You must understand everyone has a story, and I hope mine can help you jumpstart your life and move you in the direction of healing. Are you willing to be those jumper cables for the next person?

So, sit back and enjoy this book. This book will be breathtaking and insightful about my life. I recognized that many people claim they know but have no earthly idea about me. Yes, I will admit you heard gossip, some truths, and a lot of speculations.

I need you to open your mind and take away any previous thoughts you might have about me. If you allow your prejudgment of me and what you think this ride about to be about. You will be doing yourself a great disservice. You about to be moved, if you knew of me, well you about to honestly know me. Redemption is about to make you rethink any and everything you may have heard about me.

Redemption is about to take flight. Get you some popcorn, put your seatbelt on and let us take this trip together. Let's vibe together.

First, I think it is very vital to understand the difference between forgiveness and redemption. A lot of people have the meaning of the two words confused or think they are the same. **Forgiveness** is a choice made by the party who an offense was committed against. **Redemption** is the release from the consequences of the offense for the person who committed the offense. In a secular circumstance, an offender can be **forgiven** while not receiving **redemption**.

Contents

Foreword v

Redemption vi

Introduction viii

Chapter 1: Loosing Myself 1

Chapter 2: The Redemption of Friendship 17

Chapter 3: What Is Redemption of Love? 33

Chapter 4: What is The Redemption of the Parent? 49

Chapter 5: What is Your Redemption Story? 63

Chapter 1: Loosing Myself

What does redemption mean to you? When I breakdown the meaning of redemption, I think it gives me the opportunity to right a wrong. The evil or wrong I have done to a person(s) or a situation that I involved myself in.

REDEMPTION IN THE COMMUNITY

In 1993, I started sneaking out of my grandmother's house, and I lived in the basement. I would hear different noises coming from somewhere. The sounds of people, music, car doors slamming, and car tires burning rubber in the streets. I peeked out the windows on certain nights each week, so Thursday, Friday, and Saturday were the nights. The funny thing about me running to the window on those nights, I could not see anything but my neighbors' house.

Jones' family stayed next to my grandmother's house. If you're from Starkville, Mississippi, you know Kirk, Melvin, Mary, and Tasha Jones. It was their mother's house and during these times, Tasha Jones stayed there with her mom. Tasha and I had a great relationship, she would become a close friend of mine, and we shared many beautiful moments together. They were my family. I have a lot of respect and love for the Jones family.

Okay, nothing is going on at the Jones' yard, and I would tell myself, *"Boy you must be hearing stuff."* I would return to watching T.V., just lay there talking to myself or play basketball, thinking I was MJ (Michael Jordan). Those were the days, and I mean the days; I had no worries in the world but too much time on my hand. *I would later discover; I was not crazy at all.*

As the weeks passed by, once again Thursday, Friday, and Saturday night, I am hearing the music, people, and cars down the street. Okay, I know, I am not crazy, there is something going on. I go and put my clothes on and slide out the back door. Before I did, I went upstairs and checked on my grandmother, as I usually did every night. I knew her schedule anyway, and 9:00 pm was her bedtime. My baby is sleeping, cool, so this is my chance to check out the scene.

I walked out the back door and seen Tasha sitting on the porch. *"Pooh, what are you doing,"* Tasha asked me? *"Nothing; I was bored and seen you on the porch, so I came out and just chill with you for a few minutes."* This was the first lie I told Tasha, and it was plenty more to come. Later the lies would stop because Tasha knew I was into the street, and that was it. She never encouraged nor agreed with what I decided to do.

Tasha kept talking and for anyone who knows her, she had a lot to say about a lot of things in the hood. She kept talking and I kept pretending to listen. Nodding my head every once and a while. I did not hear one thing she was saying that night. My sole purpose for coming out of the back door was the see some action. And did I see some action!!! *Wow,* and I said to myself, *this a whole new world.* I knew it, and I witnessed it firsthand now; people, cars, music, and eventually I would discover that there were a lot of drugs being sold.

I stood there just watching; Tasha just talking, and I me just fake listening to her voice in the background. It amazed me how these people were just out partying with no issues. I had no clue to what was truly going on, but it looked much better than looking at a 13" black and white T.V. with 5 channels. I continued to watch the different activities, and a joyful feeling ran through my body. I knew from that moment; I wanted and needed this in my life.

This was an inflection point in my life, so weeks later, my life would never be the same again for decades to come. An inflection point is a personal decision(s) or events that will alter their life.

This decision can relate to your education, career, sex, but in my case, I was about to enter the dark world of drug selling, money, cars, and countless women.

Okay, I had seen enough; I went and sat on the steps, and yeah, Tasha is still talking, but I started daydreaming. I thought *I will take my dreams, turning them into thousands of dollars.*

I finally left Tasha's porch. Back at home I just lay in bed with my mind is racing. For some reason, the music and voices were getting louder and louder. The battle was on. "What battle?" You might be asking yourself? The battle of the mind. How could I live this double life without my grandmother and father finding out? I had to think in a manner I never did before. This was the crazy conversation my 13-year-old self was having with himself. How foolish of me? But hey, I wanted it, so I had to plan.

Every week was typical for me until Thursday night came and the same routine down the street. I do not remember why, but I did not participate in football that year. My Ace, Jaysun Minor, my best friend, was upset with me. You had to get to know him. He could not stay mad at you long. Later, I would discover I made a terrible decision missing time with my friends. A small arrangement in your life could be a life-changing moment.

I continued to wait until my grandmother went to sleep, and then head to the Jones' house to sit and watch. It was always the same thing, some of the same people, *"wow"* I said to myself, "this *is the life."* Weeks passed. I would just watch and admire the things I saw right before my eyes. I told myself *I cannot move on to the situation yet. Not yet, I must continue to watch and wait for the right moment or person.* I just waited and waited.

I got to thinking to myself and started analyzing the environment around me. The setup did not register to my mind back twenty plus years ago; what happened to the neighborhood? My neighborhood consists of only four homes and schools. Yes, I remember construction going on, and then apartments coming up below our house. One of the funniest things behind our house was the cemetery, and some people would freak out. But, for me standing by the back fence and looking over the graveyard, reading the people's names, and *wondering what happened to them* was peaceful. I would ask my grandmother and father about some of the names. My dad always had a story about most of the people. The cemetery was a familiar place for my family. In 1941, my grandfather and grandmother started Mississippi Funeral Service. I heard so many bold and moving stories about my grandfather. Burton Lawrence Robinson was from Charlotte, NC.

Nancy G. Robinson was my heart, angel, educator, cook, spiritual leader, my prayer warrior, my speechwriter, my comfort, my diva, and my world, and my grandmother. I never have and will not ever meet another beautiful soul like my grandmother; she was my daily solace.

Let us move ahead in the story. Back to those Thursday nights in the neighborhood. This particular Thursday was different, and the moment I had been waiting for so many weeks. Finally, the time and place were just right for me. I jump off the concert wall and almost broke my ankle. I see a specific car and face.

"What's up? What's up? What the hell are you doing out here? You better take your butt back home." "Who you talking to?" I answered back. *You!!* Like a teenager, who thinks they're grown, and I do not have to go anywhere.

I sat back and was stunned by the scene; it was nothing compared to what I thought I saw from the hill. The atmosphere was more in-depth; it was a lot of moving parts, and people were everywhere. I do not think you understand me, a 14-year-old kid from a small town in Mississippi, and he is supposed to be under the covers sleeping; he is watching this movie play out. I am talking about dice games, women selling themselves, weed smoke in the air, crack cocaine, guns, and people walking around mouth twisted up looking like zombies.

The traffic was flowing back and forth, cars just in and out within 2 minutes, so I was like *darn,* they move through faster than

Wendy's drive thru. People walking in and out of particular apartments and from behind the building. I was in shock, but at the same token, I felt very comfortable and at ease with the situation. I stood there for another hour or so just watching the people. I knew certain people there from around the neighborhood, park, or only in town.

Eventually, I approached the same person I spoke with initially when I walked down the hill. He was a family member of mine, and I will call him Black Knight. Black Knight was a cold dude and heartless to a certain degree. But if he was down with you, you had a friend for life. This dude was a born hustler, got it from ground zero. He was a student of the game and became a big player in the game.

"What's up, cuz;

"What is that you selling?

"Boy, I thought I told you to take your butt home."

"Cuz, what is that? I see you making some money."

This was my first-time seeing crack cocaine. I had no clue such a small object could rip apart so many lives. I was not going anywhere, so when things would slow down, he was educating me. I was about to see the different sizes of crack rock. These guys are running this stuff like a business, and everyone has their own consumers.

I ask Black Knight, "how much you got now?"

"An 8ball."

"What is an 8ball?"

He told me, and I backed off because business was rolling, and I did not want to be in his way. Well, I was already in the way, and had to fall back and watch.

The conversation restarted, and I was informed if you spend a certain amount of money, you will double your money. The product must be right, and you will make money. Black Knight said, "it is over with, and it's times for you to go home." I started to walk away but instead chilled by the stop sign that led to my house. I see the lookout people, I see sex behind buildings, I see smokers hit the pipe, and I now see a way to get some money. This night I knew, I wanted to be a part of this world; oh man, I was cool with it. I already knew I would have the money, and I already had some money stacked up. I did some work at the funeral home to earn money, plus I received extra pay for planting the garden we had on Saturday and other odd jobs.

When I look back on this decision, being honest, I know it was terrible. But it was a great decision as well. I should have waited, but God knew I would go down this path in life. I can imagine some of your faces with me say that it was a great decision as well. Allow me to explain. I have met some of the smartest people in the streets, and a lot of the people I met in the streets showed me more and gave me free information that my family did not give me. The knowledge I have now will continue to take me places.

I need you to open your mind and understand how critical thinking plays in the dark world. And I need you to exercise this activity, so you can appreciate the journey. More importantly, I need to open your mind and erase the false narrative you had about ex-drug dealers or anyone that was not living the way you deem as right for someone else life. If it was not for this world and my willingness to embrace and stay true to the people and the game. I would not be able to do a lot of the things I am currently doing in life. And all the things I do now are positive.

I was this kid who was lost, low self-esteem barely had friends; I did not know if people like me for me or who my dad was in life. So, the decision was not the right choice in life; it had me chasing money, women, clothes, fake dreams and fake people, and places. This world will take people's freedom, and addicts are formed on both sides of the equations. Furthermore, I would like to take you on a ride for a minute. The world of drugs, the world of darkness, the world of helping demolish your own community and countless other cities across the globe.

It is so many levels to the drug world—the street-level hustlers, which 98% of drug dealers start. And everyone's goal is to become the head of their own organization. Let me be very clear, this world is not just for "GHETTO PEOPLE/ THUG PEOPLE" as most have been classified to be. If you think drug dealing is only for thug people and low-income housing residents, you are sadly mistaken for the truth. I know lawyers, teachers, coaches, judges, officers, doctors, administrators, and the list goes on.

The journey for me was crazy. I always tried to be very secretive about my life, and I had no choice because of my father. As years went on, I went from street level, trafficking, and just sitting back and making orders. Please, I am not saying each step was easy, nor did I not make it to one level and take a step back. The drug world is a deadly, unloyalty, and a daily game of Russian Roulette. The drug business has some good stand-up guys and women in this game. I was always shown and taught good business practice goes further than any crap. You must stand on your word. And I have been in situations and witness some circumstances where Your Word is the only way you made it home alive.

Many self-employers and employees do not make it out of this world, but on the flip side, I know many ex-drug dealers who run some of the biggest companies in the world. You won't ever know it, and that person could be your close friend, husband, wife, boss, lawyer, football coach, or even the President of the United States. I know people who do not compare a drug dealer and a business owner to the same people. Some of these major dealers have become users and some of the biggest users have become drug kingpins. The majority of people who decide to become dealers are forced into this life or you have someone like me, I just enjoyed hustling. I know you're thinking to yourself, everyone has a choice, and you are correct, but do you know their options.

I had an early addiction to that lifestyle, and it was not about the flashy life because I had two parents who were flashy in their own legal lanes. My dad was the King of the flashy life. But his life was legal. For some reason, I just like the lifestyle, and the people were cool. Yes, I've could've continued to play sports, going to school, church, and whatever else I had to be doing at that age. I saved my money and was able to buy my first pack (drugs to sell). At this time, I must blend in with the other dealers, plus at the same time found my own clients. I was doing fine. I played sports, going to school, and just start living a double life.

One Thursday night, I was walking on the west side, and my teammates spotted me selling drugs, and my cover was blown amongst certain people. He told my friend girl because he wanted to bang her and that was weird to me. I never was taught a guy should speak negatively on another man just to get sex from his girl. As a small-time hustler, which was cool with me, I was not in the position to raise no noise, so my dad would know about me. Before my dad would know, I had to watch out for my cousin Ray, and he would tell the whole family.

The idea of my grandmother and aunt Linda, who I adored then and even still, knowing, would have crushed me. She was the attorney of the family and years later told me how she disliked drug dealers. To be honest, my aunt Linda is the person I wanted to be like, a lawyer. You cannot out debate me, and I live on facts. Plus, I can make you believe your truth is nothing but a lie. I miss that calling, but God had a bigger plan for my life.

As time went by, I started to hang out with older people who were doing the same thing I was doing. This was the move I had to make to get a full grasp of the situation. The knowledge was outstanding, and it helped that I had excellent listening skills and never talked out of place. I was learning the art of selling. The older guys always question me on; why? Why would you be out here with us, and you got it made? They had no clue about my life behind closed doors. That is the world we will always live in; people always think they know your situation and barely know their own conditions.

I would take breaks during football season and run wild the other months. My life was fresh; I was shopping weekly, buying my own stuff, but I could not buy everything; I had to hide my other life. My main concern was to continue to be seen only as of the FUNERAL HOME MAN'S SON. And, you know how life goes; everything done in the dark will come to light.

The life I knew until this point was about to change forever, and I was not ready for it. My grandmother left for the summer in 1994 to visit my aunt and never returned. In my little brain, I was delighted, and the summer was hot on the hill. Parties, girls, fake friends, weed-smoking, money, and drugs to sell. But I did not understand until years later the impact it would have on my development as a person. I was not giving the option to go with my grandmother, and it was not even talked about with me.

I believe my dad stayed at the house with me for a month if that long. Therefore, imagine a 15-year-old kid, no guidance, no curfew, money is not a topic nor problem, some drug money, older friends, and women, and so much of time. The mixer will not come out well for a kid in that situation.

So, I remember months later, I was informed my grandmother and aunt were coming home, and I knew I would be moving to Jackson. We had a wonderful time together and it was like she never left me. The days were dwindling down, and it was time for them to leave and return home. I had my suitcases ready to go because I just knew she was coming to get her baby boy. If anyone was going to make sure I was okay and no worries, my grandmother always made me feel safe and protected. Nope, we sat at the dinner table, and my aunt Linda talked to me about life.

She was very clear to me about her expectations of me, and she was very clear about my intelligence, how I could become anything I dream of being. She went on to say; how she has a strong dislike for drug dealers, and I am thinking to myself, this is not how the story supposed to go.

How did the tides turn that quick? She used her lawyer tactics on me; just to juice me up for this speech, it is not about a banana. I am thinking we were about to discuss the rules of me moving to Jackson, and she is talking about drugs. I do not want to do this; I just wanted to be saved from this life. I can recall while we are talking, and I look at the door here comes a crack head. So, I gave him the cutthroat gesture, and he left the walkway. I realize I wasn't going anywhere and just left behind again; I wanted no more part of my so-called good life. I hated to see my grandmother and aunt leave. As usual, they told me they loved me and see me another time. But they loaded up in my aunt's gold Camry, and that was it.

I cried and cried. I just wanted to be wanted by someone. It is hard for a child to not feel wanted by anyone in his family. That moment combined with everything else I dealt with until that Sunday, and I became a cold-hearted beast. I picked myself up, and it was the usual thing for me to do in life. I had to learn at a young age, no one will ever be around nor there for you. This was the beginning of my abandonment issues, and it will haunt me for the next 25 years of my life. So, it is time to get deeper into the game.

I started traveling to get drugs, and I was during everything in the drug game; besides, snitching, robbing people, just anything that would be considered disloyalty to the crew. I learned the hard way that loyalty is not always a receptacle.

Furthermore, I was making connections with many different places, but just did I know the prices, and the consistency was across the river, Columbus, Mississippi. I finally found the guy; I could trust and make things happen. He had it all and everything I needed. I was able to cut out the middleman and deal directly with the man with drugs. I will call him the C-Town connect; he was a laid-back guy, and to be honest, we were looking for the same thing. C-Town wanted to add more territory to his business, and I needed my own outlet.

In this game, like any other business, it is all about the numbers. In any business, its cost, quality of the product, what makes your product stand out, and what is my profit margin. PERIOD. As we talked and became more comfortable with each other, we both discovered this will be a great business move. I would buy some products, and some would be on credit. When I say credit just like in a store, you want a particular item out of Walmart; if your credit (WORD IN THE STREET) is right, you can get what you want. And you would be charged a little extra.

I know you probably asking yourself, why is he going into details about this underworld? I am sharing how you can go from a local joe to spreading drugs to numerous communities in a blink of an eye. So, we had a great relationship, until I made a huge mistake, I introduced C-Town to a friend. They started dealing and making moves, but with this friend, I learned everyone close to you is not solid. And they will dirty the game and possibly your name. Eventually, their relationship soured, and I ended up on a cross, which I had no idea about. But I worked things out, and we had a great relationship until C-Town went to federal prison.

This world took me to many different cities and states, the Upstate New York area, Chicago, Louisiana, Alabama, Georgia, Milwaukee, California, and Memphis, Tennessee. I met some wonderful people; I encountered some dangerous cutthroat people that viewed life that was not worth it.50 cent. But that is a part of the lifestyle.

PLEASE, I REPEAT PLEASE DON'T ENTER INTO THIS LIFE. IT ISN'T WHAT YOU NEED, BUT AT THE SAME TOKEN, I UNDERSTAND SOME PEOPLE DOESN'T HAVE A DIFFERENT OPTION. YOU ARE SAYING, YES, THEY DO!!!!!

HOW DO YOU KNOW THEIR CHOICES?

The next 25 years, but not a whole 25 years because I took some breaks in between those years. I have sold drugs, or I had my hands in receiving money from drug transactions always my whole life. This is a sad but actual reality of what my life had been until now. I learned a lot, I have seen a lot, and I know a lot of people who have been on drugs. I know doctors, lawyers, judges, teachers, pastors, and some high-ranked political figures, who smoke crack or snorted cocaine. If I were the type of person to name drop, you would be amazed by those individuals. But this book is not about calling out people. This book is about Redemption, my story of redemption. And what I went through as a kid, plus the things I have done and will continue to do to redeem myself.

The misconception about people, who sell or the user of drugs, both have an addiction and play a significant role in destroying the community. Yes, one would debate his or her side of the story, but both are killing the community. My own view on it is the dealer, who is feeding the community with the drugs. Those dealers are taking monies from the users' family, household, infecting the community with drugs that could kill anyone.

I need to think about the crack babies that were born in the communities, home invasions, cars, and store break-in. The list of evil that comes from being a drug dealer or user is off the charts. Furthermore, when incarcerations occur, men and women who leave their kids behind, who is going to help the parent that is left behind to fend for him/her and the kids. The mother or father cannot do their part in the household because the drugs have taking them over and the dealer whose life is centered around drug dealing. The dealer is an immediate problem in the community just as much as the user.

HOW DO WE FIX THIS?

This is where the redemption part plays a significant role in communities across the world. As a drug user, you must get some help, which can consist of drug rehabilitation programs, meetings, a program that will give you insight and help redirect your mind. The drugs have made become dependent on a substance that you are chasing from the first hit. These selfish behaviors must be removed from your life because your family, kids, friends, and community need you. The impact of your decision can reach so many people and make you feel worthy again. Once you receive help, it is imperative you got back to the community and talk with the other addicts you might have left behind or new users. You can speak their same language; your experiences will resonate in their souls, and they will feel the passion in your voice.

The different nonprofit organizations that need former drug users to deliver encouraging messages. How many churches can use your talents, but do whatever is necessary to change the community? As a drug dealer, you have the same obligations to return to the community and clean it up. I need you to think about the dysfunction, crime, thefts, and possibly killing that occurs. It falls on your lap as well, oh no, oh yes, because you were there to distribute crack cocaine.

In retrospect, you need to have the same energy and eagerness to encourage the next set of drug dealers to stop and change the culture. The next move is getting a job, getting a trade, further your education, or anything productive. Yes, I understand the people who will say you do not know my option, and you are exactly right; I do not know them. I do know, a person will rather stay out of prison and take the longer route than years behind bars. This move is the best play in the game, and you do not want to put yourself in a situation to become a snitch.

WHY YOU SAY THAT BERT?

A lot of people talk that talk but cannot handle prison. A rat cannot help the community in any way. Men, women, and kids who make the decision to become part of the underworld are mostly by force and some by choice. It will come a time when your loyalty is put to the test; do I tell on the next man, or do I take this time. Some people cannot think quickly and that is a needed skill because the wrong words can get you killed. The movies and YouTube videos do not tell the full story.

I looked forward to redeeming myself within my community; I helped destroyed, and other cities in different states. I have been a part of a ministry called O'BLAC in Dallas, Texas, which helped bring people off the streets into the church. I started Robinson Youth Foundation, the foundation teaches kids the basic drills in football, but the focus is teaching boys to become kings. We stress the importance of education, financial literacy, reading, credit, writing a resume, filling out applications, and other areas of becoming a man.

I worked on the board that started the first annual Starkville Cook-Off that raised money to clean up the neighborhoods. The event also helps save the King Center and provide equipment for youth sports. The King Center helps people obtain their GED and provide after school care for kids. I started a podcast, Mississippi Vibes with Bert, it is a weekly talk show and a platform to help people change their lives. I had various guests on the show; former mayor, first African American Police Chief in Starkville, Mississippi, President of NAACP, former NFL first-round draft pick, Black Panther Leader, doctors, lawyers, and the list goes on. This is another form of **REDEMPTION.**

I had several conversations with some people that I had introduced to the world of drugs; a lot of them were able to avoid prison sentences, and some had to pay the price. As we talked, I made a point to apologize to them for leading them into a life of danger, sleepless nights, and always looking over their shoulders. I made sure; I gave them alternative routes to take. Each person I knew what their skills were so, I made it a significant point to stress this skill set that God blessed you is one of the ways you can go. We had an in-depth dialogue about how this new life is not going to be easy nor will it be an overnight mental transaction.

I want you to understand; guys and ladies I talked with have 10-20 years of this lifestyle engrained in their minds. Therefore, their journey into this new world isn't easy for some, I would like you to picture yourself fighting to stop eating certain foods, losing weight, and leaving a relationship that's bad for you but you're together since high school.

Our talks get deeper when we have to discuss the money factors, I'm asking these people to imagine making $2000-$3000/ weekly as their own boss to go get a job or start their own business, and their weekly pay drops 75%-85%. I understand I have been there; I know how the struggle will be. I know the drawbacks; I will get from them. But I have the same obligations to get them to leave the game as I did to get them to enter the dark world of drug dealers.

I've been successful with over half of the people I talked with, and that is okay because I did not expect each one to just say cool; I'M READY. Some went cold turkey like I finally did, some left and went back to make a couple of plays (deals). But they are right now, legit. I still check to make sure they are doing fine; their families are okay. They are my family. I have always been a family person because I did not have that bond with my family. My mother's side of the family that is.

This is a form of **REDEMPTION.**

I went back to get the people and their families; I lead into this world. I felt when I was in the drug world, it was my place to show them how to get money, so I must show them how to go legit and build a profitable empire legally. Just picture your people and their families are healthy, God-fearing people, thriving in their communities, reaching back, and guiding other young men and women to not fall into the darkness. Wow. What a beautiful feeling? It brings TEARS OF JOY to my soul. I never envision having such a moment, my wrongs, but God knew.

It is all about reaching back, it's all about building others, it's all about life, it's all about love, it's all about peace, and most of all, IT'S ALL ABOUT REDEEMING YOURSELF.

The steps you will need to take for REDEMPTION: happen in the Streets.

1. Stop destroying your community.
2. If you can start a foundation or join a foundation that is bringing change.
3. Reach One Teach One; help bring a person(s) out of street life.
4. Also, bring awareness to the injustice that is happening within your community.
5. Be a leader for change.

Chapter 2: The Redemption of Friendship

When I think of friendship, I see two people, male, or female, who share an unbreakable and unshakable bond. A bond that has its ups and downs. But a relationship that will survive battles and wars. As I dig deeper, True friends do not care where you are from, nor what you possibly have been through; it's about the mutual affection, understanding, respect, and loyalty the two people share.

A true friendship turns into brotherhood or sisterhood; either way, real friends are family members without a birth certificate. I do not think a lot of people understand the core value of friendships; I believe it is something people say, just like when you walk into a room, you say "Hello." It is a natural thing to do. So, you have been around a person, you hung out a few times and boom, we friends?

To some people, its major, it's a union, its life, and death, it's their alliance, they hurt, you hurt, they cry, you cry, it's not a game, and we don't cross each other as friends (Family). It's a code we live by, regardless of if we go months and don't hear from each other because of life situations, but when we do talk or see each other's, it's like, we are picking up from the last time we spoke or seen each other. Let us not forget some, well, I cannot say what they do, because my mind does not operate in such a manner. I can speak on it, I experienced from so-called friends, we refer to them as acquaintances.

An acquaintance is someone who you just met, just knowledge of the person, but it's nothing near a friendship. Yes, in life, we try hard sometimes to make people our friends when we need to keep them in the acquaintance lane. Those people can be helpful, they might have knowledge of someone, who fix on cars, selling discounted tires, can fix your AC Unit, can wash your car, and some acquaintance is good people, but they won't be the friend you need to be a part of your personal life. In some cases, I have seen where they are great for someone who is a friend to you, but not your cup of tea. If you know what I mean.

I wanted to touch on that, so you can understand and not confuse the two lanes in life. It is a massive difference. When I was younger, I did not know the difference. You would hear your parents or other family members say that it is your acquaintance and not your friend, but it was rarely an explanation behind the statement. Back to the actual discussion of this chapter, REDEEMING A FRIENDSHIP, I have been blessed with some fantastic long-lasting friendships. I have some friends, well as I stated, I see them as my family. I would go to battle with them any day and every day.

The first real friend I ever had was with MY ACE, JAYSUN E. MINOR. He was a gentle giant. He had a smile that would change your mood in a second. His heart was so pure, and his love for you was unquestionable. This dude could play basketball, baseball, and football; we grew up playing all three sports together for years. And his talents went beyond he was a master drummer and singer. Jaysun was smart; also, his mom was a teacher, so you know the rest about his educational drive.

We spent countless hours and days together growing up on the hill. No, Jaysun was not from that area; he was a country boy, he grew up in the Sessum area of Starkville, Mississippi. Mrs. Minor, who was Jaysun's mom, taught school across the street from the house I grew up in. I later found out at my grandmother's funeral; my grandmother was Jaysun's mom mentor in the teaching field. Our families have been connected for years.

Jaysun, my ace, I can remember a time when we played baseball, and the kid we went to school with, Michael Pan, was pitching against us. I smile when I think about this, me, Jaysun and Clarence Townsend. We were the three-headed monsters on the baseball team, and for many years, we played baseball together. It was like picking your poison. No matter how hard the opposing pitchers tried, we were going to work them over.

On this day, Michael had his game on, and if I am not mistaking, this was our first time seeing him that season. I know for me, I only seen a curveball on T.V., but I think I am speaking for them as well. Hell, I know for sure the other kids did not; they could not hit to save us. Just joking, just joking, not seriously, a few players just had to fill out the roster.

So, I think the first time in history, he was able to strike us all out the first time around. It was killing me inside that this 5'1, 130 if that was striking us out. I was the kid who had one of the worse attitudes, and I always spoke my mind regardless. I would allow my mood to make me lose my focus on the task in front of me. I never wanted to let my teammates, friends, and family down. I felt this was one of those days, I was facing adversity and could not do anything. My Ace could sense different things within me, we hang out together countless hours during the week. I can see myself zoning in on his movements as a pitcher.

I am focused so hard I see the muscles in his legs moving. So, we back up, we down by a run or two, and it is our time, THE ORIGINAL BIG 3, yes that was us before any professional team forms their BIG 3. Jaysun figured it out, he called us over, "Pooh (that's me), Clarence," in his usual low-key. "Yea, what's up," "It's dropping, man I do not have time for this mess," I said in my hotheaded tone. I used other words, but for the sake of kids' reading this, I will keep it there. "Pooh, listen and calm down," he said, "We got him."

"Okay, what is up," that's Clarence, he was always calm and laid back, a silent warrior, and it was no question in his talent and leadership. "The ball is dropping, when it gets to the front of the plate, the ball just drops," Jasysun tells us. Drops, man what? Yes, drop, okay, cool. I walk back to the fence, and I think he can feel my eyes ripping through his soul.

My anger towards Michael is as at an all-time high. He does not know it, but the ball game has just turned around. Clarence gets on by a walk, and now it's me and this 5'1, 130 pounds kid. The whole time as I am walking to the batter box, I can hear Ace say, THE BALL DROPS, THE BALL DROPS.

I never adjusted my stance before; I was taught by my cousin Kenyon self, who was my baseball idea growing up. He took many hours out to show me about baseball and how to hit the ball. The hand placement, how far to stand off the plate, the strike zone, and I used to travel to all his games. But, this time, I had to come up in the batter box near the tip of the plate. I had to catch the ball before it DROPPED. I waited and I even got behind in the count, so once that happens in baseball, the pitcher will go to his money pitch. I know what is coming; I had watched his form, his movements when it is time to throw the curveball.

Ok, its 2-2 count, he is looking at the fake signal; I am very relaxed; Ace already told me the ball drops. The release, I slowed the ball down in my mind and eyes, I could see the spin, the name on the ball, it's moving very slow and boom. A line drive back up the middle, the Easton 36" bat I carried collided with the ball, and I tried to knock his head off with the ball. A double the whole game just changed, and we ended up winning. My Ace helped us adjust and secure another victory.

We went on and spent more hours, days, weeks, months, and years together. When you see one, you saw the other. We shared locker rooms and showers together. I was the power forward, Ace was the center, I played third base, Ace played first base. I played right guard; he was the right tackle. We had each other's back until our junior year in high school; life throws us another curveball. Ace focused on school, music, his new girlfriend, and doing things a typical teenager our age did. Me on the other hand, I wanted to sell drugs, more money, cars, clothes, smoking weed, and anything your mind can imagine.

I just gave you a blink of a few years of our friendship. I have plenty of stories about our friendship and others. But I will dive into the good stuff. How do you redeem yourself from a bond you abandoned? You decided to take another path, or it might be a childish misunderstanding that leads to years of no contact or knowledge about your friend's life.

REDEMPTION ASPECT OF THIS FRIENDSHIP

Let us fast forward to 2013; I was in our hometown of Starkville, Mississippi. I just traveled from Dallas, Texas, area and after making the eight-hour drive, wanted some Chinese food. At that time, China Garden in Starkville had the best Chinese food. That is just my opinion. As I entered the building, I always scan the whole place or any building I walk into. People who know me, I like to set myself, I do not care to be bunched up table by table. Ok, I spot where I am going to show the hostess, where I would like to be seated. And, wow, I see Ace, my best friend, I have not seen this guy since 1997 or 1998.

Ace, he replied, *"man, what's up, boy"* he reached out his hand. But something is not right; he cannot see me. His hand did not connect with my hand. My Ace, my dawg, my homie, my partner, my right-hand man, my right tackle, my center, my drummer, my and I can go on and on using different adjectives to describe him. He introduced me to his beautiful wife, Kalie Minor, who is a strong God-fearing woman. I met a lot of women, on a personal level, or just through family and friends. Kalie Minor is one of the strongest women I know to this day. I SALUTE HER. I sat down, she said, I heard so much about you and I finally get to meet you. Ace was just smiling, lol, showing that gap. Jaysun had a smile that could turn a gloomy day into the brightest day you could ever see.

We talked, caught up on old times, shared old stories, discussed my dad and his mom, Mrs. Minor. He told me about his kids, which he had three daughters, I talked about my kids. It is like we never away from each other for the past 13 years. A lot had changed in our lives, but one thing about Jaysun, he always knew we would reconnect on the other side and be stronger together as men.

Ace, "what's up, Pooh, man" "I have this football camp, and I want you to speak." Okay, I will do it. Just let me know, and I will be there. I gave him the rundown of the camp and how it will be different than any other camps around the world, not just in the state of Mississippi. Most of all, we just enjoyed our meal together and I hugged him, kissed him on his forehead and let him now, I will not be leaving your side anymore in life.

I felt so bad, he has gone through so many obstacles in life, and I was not by his side. I finally made it to the car. I cried like a newborn baby needing some food or a nap. From that day forward, we talked and texted each other weekly. He did a phenomenal job speaking to the kids at the youth football camp. He became my prayer warrior and introduced me to so many scriptures in the Bible that told stories about the journeys we took in life. I apologized to him for not being around and countless other actions I have done throughout the years. I started working with people who lost their eyesight and gave up on life.

I went back into coaching; I started with youth football and basketball, those two of the sports we loved. I changed some areas of my life. I read more, and I began to reevaluate my life in any way possible. His family moved to Charlotte, we started to hang out. I had a family in charlotte, so we back slick again. I invited his family over for a Christmas dinner and I was so delighted to share that experience with him. I did not talk much; I just sat back and enjoyed the moment. I never wanted Ace and the family to leave. My phone rings, Ace- *"what's up man, I am going to put something on the grill; I want you and your family to come over.* "Hell *yeah, I am coming,* we will be there, and I was early and ahead of time. He was doing great, his family good. I was doing good on my side. We grilled, we told stories, we laughed, Ace and

I put some extra sauce on our stories; also, they were real stories, but you must add spice to any good storyline. It is the Mississippi way of doing things.

I got my guy back; we are rolling now. I was able to express with his face to face about the things that happened in my life. I have always been the type of dude who refrains from bringing my friends into the lifestyle; I was living in the streets. I made that decision when I was in high school. It just a respect level you got to have in the dark world. Plus, I knew their makeup, and if I did, I felt I would be exposed to my family. We continue to grow our relationship, we shared different events together, and we were just the same best friends since little league sports. But did we know in a few months, our life would change forever, and this was not good.

The last time I think I physically saw Ace was at a surprise party I had in Charlotte, NC. The phone conversations, texts, and Facebook exchanges never stop, so we are good, and we are making plans to do things in the future. He was overjoyed about his life. He was about to become a grandfather, another daughter graduating high school and college, he was working, helping individuals in the church and Charlotte area period.

We are working together to Redeem our friendship/relationship. It is a beautiful thing, and Ace call me; I missed his call on several occasions and text messages, work had me going, and when I called back.

What's up, Ace, "*man, you hard to catch up with,*"
'*No, brother, this work got me going and trying to get things right to make that move your way.*" As the conversation carried on, he was explaining to me, he knew this guy who wanted to start a youth organization with him. Jaysun told him it was a great idea, but we need to talk with my Ace and see what he got to say. I asked him, you said to him that, yes, I told him, you knew how to put it together and we going to do it as a team. Jaysun and I laid

out the groundwork and what the mission of the organization would be.

I explain to him this will be a power move and put our name in the history books and leave a legacy our kids would be proud of. If you had, and if you know Jaysun, he is a Godly man and does not make moves without discussion with God nor his wife. I was thrilled my guy recognized my talents and knew I was the man for the job. That is **REDEMPTION.** Being able to regain your friend's trust is a top priority, not that we did anything to lose or damage our confidence in the friendship.

So, game on, it is time to go to work. I spoke with the other person involved in the situation. I made sure he knew that everything had to be discussed with Jaysun and agreed upon by him as well. We are working, we are talking, we are doing it, and the launch date is 2020 for the organization. The organization is going to grow into the largest, most successful, durable, thriving, and result built the program in Charlotte and surrounding areas.

On March 31st, 2020, which was a Tuesday morning, I was working and talking, my phone rang. *"Good morning:"* good morning, I replied, *"you heard about Jaysun,"* no ma'am. *"You need to call his wife; he in the hospital."* I follow the instruction I was just giving, and I called. *"Hello, hey, what's up baby? He isn't doing good,"* she said, *"what's going on,"* I asked. *"We think he got the coronavirus. I brought him here Saturday, and he is not doing good."* We both crying like two babies looking for a snack.

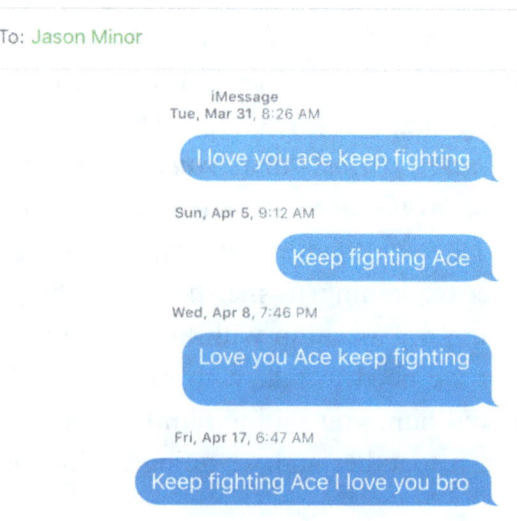

To: Jason Minor

> I love you to death. I need you to continue to fight. This shit ain't right Ace we have too much life left to live and inspire people.
> I apologize for not being there I know in your heart you know I love you and never had or will have a Ace in my life like you.
>
> We done things that will go to the gravel with us. I will do my best to look out for your wife kids and grandkid.
>
> I will from this day forward dedicate my life to you forever.
>
> Love you to death. Love you I hope you able to read this but I know you will when you come home
>
> God knows what's best
>
> Love you Ace

His wife and I continue to text and texting every day from this point on. We told stories, laughed, and cried. I prayed heavily for him. As you saw above, I was texting him, I just wanted to hear his voice again, I wanted my Ace back, we have too much ahead of us. I am thinking to myself, I got relationships to fix with my family and God, now you want me to tackle this also. **OKAY, I AM BUILT FOR THIS LIFE.**

The next two and half weeks the fight was on, Jaysun has overcome so many obstacles, battles, life-changing scenarios and live to see another day, weeks, months, and years. In my mind, if anyone can accomplish this task and destroy this beast, My Ace can. He would show progress and he would go back a few steps; he would show improvement and he would go back to dependability mode.

Wow, this is hard sitting here typing this portion of the book and still just unbelievable to me. God has given me certain spirits, I can feel things, I can see them before it happens. I am speaking about weeks or months in advance.

Fri, Mar 13, 11:36 AM

> What's up God has put it on my heart to inform Us that something is coming down the pipeline that will rock our family. Don't know what it is but it's something
> Love y'all and be safe

Pam

 Thanks!

Once again, you can see from the picture above, I felt this coming ahead of time. That message rang true twice for me this year. I thought it was something about our family personally, which would have involved all my siblings, but the message was directly for me from God. God was telling me; my *son is about to*

experience a life-changing movement, and I need you ready for this journey.

It is a raining day, I do not feel like going to work, but I got to get this money. I do not want to be here, well, let me see what excuse I can come up with to leave this place, my thoughts that day. Monday, April 20, 2020, at 8:31 a.m., my phone ringing, Kalie-Ace Wife, the name comes up on the screen, that is her name in my phone. I started walking towards the break room, tears are pouring down my face and I say hello, hollering, *"He GONE POOH, HE GONE;" DAMN* was all I could fix my mouth to speak. She explained to me what happened and how we at this point in our lives.

To: **Jason Minor**

Mon, Apr 20, 8:43 AM

I know you fought I know you give it your all I know you fought I know you give it your all

I know you had to get home to your wife kids and grandson I know

You a solider
You can watch over them now
God needed you more

I admired you so much it's crazy

I just want to be a great husband like you I just want to be a father like you

I always wanted to play music just like you but God gifted you with that talent cause I wouldn't used it for wrong but you Ace used it to praise God and uplift His name.

Redemption: The Next Phase…

To: Jason Minor

> I admired you so much it's crazy
>
> I just want to be a great husband like you I just want to be a father like you
>
> I always wanted to play music just like you but God gifted you with that talent cause I wouldn't used it for wrong but you Ace used it to praise God and uplift His name.
>
> I will watch and take care of your family. I will I watch over and take care of your family.

> You always told me I could be whatever
>
> We owned the baseball and basketball court.

Delivered

I walked in the office and grab my things, told my supervisor, I am about to leave my brother just passed away. I will contact you when I decide to return. I drove home and cried for the rest of the day. My life has not felt right since that day. My life will not be the same anymore; everyone, who was a massive part of my life growing up, is deceased.

I want you to understand it is a time in your life when life is going to hit you like a ton of bricks. I want you to understand there is a point in your when you and a friend might lose contact for whatever reason. It happens, it is life, and some of those friends you need to lose and never try to REDEEM that relationship. It is not worth it for every situation. In this situation, redemption had to take place. We had to sow seeds back into each other and make plans together. We had so many positive moves about to happen. Jaysun and I never discussed nor dream; we both would have families in Charlotte.

Redemption is about correcting a wrong. I was dead wrong for putting streets, girls, money, a fast lifestyle before someone who just cool with being Pooh's best friend with no strings attached. I could not see that I was blinded by a fake life. My mission since I saw him and his wife at the Chinese restaurant was to make sure we never left each other's side again. We never went months or years without talking or seeing each other.

Your story can be similar or totally different, but whatever is the backstory, just make sure it you take the necessary steps to change the alignment of friendship. A few simple adult conversations will make a world of difference. The degree of wrong in your bond can be on a level where it is not going to be a smooth as our to repairing took.

Our friendship was not destroyed because I directly caused any harm, or any broken trust was involved. If you wronged them. It will take some work and time to heal that hurt. Therefore, you will have to decide is this worth it, is this person going to have a positive impact on my life. How will my life grow with this person coming back into my life? It's about growth for each party involved. This is not a one-sided coin; it cannot be mainly centered around your own selfish agenda. Being about the redeem, a true friendship is lifechanging.

The steps you will need to take for REDEMPTION to happen in your friendship.

1. You must acknowledge it has been a wrong deed(s) on your part.
2. Once you recognize the part you played in the situation. YOU MUST APOLOGIZE.
3. Be ready to openly discuss all issues that need to be resolved.
4. Listen to understand, and do not listen to reply.
5. Most of all, every day, do your part so the friendship can flourish.

The greater your assignment the longer the training. The difference between failure and success is a season. See you must be trained by God on how to keep your blessing and not lose them. See it is a price for your future. The price of your future is your life. Your life will require all of you.

In life your best friend might be that person you do not want to be around at all. This individual who is not even trying to challenge you but does. These are the people you try to avoid in life. Which in turn will be one of the biggest mistakes in make in life.

Those people are critical in our lives, it's a must you have those people who challenge you at your very core, who don't accept that just because you have a business, degree, a particular home or car that you did something amazing. They are challenging you to go way beyond that. What is your mind, body, and soul about? Remember a person who is challenging you only does so because they genuinely care and love you.

Now is always the right time to do the right thing. It's checking season, you have to check yourself. Take yourself outside of yourself and look at your life from the eyes of another person. Everyone isn't giving the same assessment of you and your actions. Shift your thinking pattern. You know small changes can have a great impact on your life.

Who or what has shackles on your mind?

Chapter 3: What Is Redemption of Love?

Redemptive Love is sacrificing yourself because of love. ... It is more profound than unconditional love. Redemption in terms of love is a sacrifice of sorts. The word redemption means there is a regaining of something in exchange for some type of payment or debt owed. When put with the word love, its meaning is magnified. Redemptive Love is sacrificing oneself because of love.

This chapter is interesting to me. This has been a roller coaster for me, love, or what I proceed to be. It took me a lot of trial and errors to finally get it right and understand the meaning of love. After various counseling sessions, time, money, and failed attempts, I got it now. But it does not mean I am going to be this perfect man. My interpretation of Redemptive Love: is a love that is vast and very pure. It goes beyond unconditional love. Redemption in terms of love is a sacrifice of sorts.

As an example, the Bible talks about Christ dying for our sins. Once sin entered our world, people were tainted, or not pure. Therefore, we could not know or be close to God, who is the purest form of love, or better yet is love itself. The act of dying for us by Christ (the giving away of something) was the only way people could be saved from their sin.

He chose to die, knowing he would die and that his death would be the exchange (redemption) and payment (a debt owed). *If* Christ had not chosen to die, then each human being would never be able to be close to God, and virtually never make it to Heaven, or have eternal salvation. And as payment or debt that would still need to be paid for all sin, each person would have to die (not in a physical sense but dying as in separation from God for eternity or being cast into Hell). Romans 6:23 of the Bible states that "the wages of sin is death..." no matter what, that debt must be paid.

Once Christ died, our sins were forgiven, and we were able to have a relationship with God (getting something in return). And, are given the ultimate gift of eternal life or having the ability to enter eternal life, or Heaven -once we die here in the physical sense. That is probably the ultimate and most well-known form of love I have ever come across. It is the best example to really show how redemptive love works. When researching that phrase or term, the Bible is mentioned extensively. That story of redemptive love really is what it means to sacrifice oneself for a greater appreciation of something else, beyond oneself.

Furthermore, when dealing with love, you got to have some faith in the situation with your mate. Faith does not mean, oh, this going to be a walk in the park, no. Faith will make it possible to happen. Faith will help you through rough patches. The success of your relationship must tie in with God as the foundation of a love affair. My journey was different than a lot of people, and my journey also can reach a lot of men. Let me explain before I got into the dynamics of love with a woman. I experienced three life-changing events, and these events would mess with my mind for years to come. The events had me questioning a lot of things within myself and the world itself. I would not subject these dysfunction events into anyone's life.

At a very young age, I was touched by a family friend, I left my mother's house before 7 years old, and by the time I was 15 years old, my grandmother left and move to Jackson, Mississippi. To this day, I could not tell you why I left my mother's house? I was able to learn when my grandmother died in 2008; why she left and never returned.

So those events shaped my mind towards a lot of things dealing with women and relationships. First, I battled with my sexuality. Do I suppose to be with women or men? Yes, I saw only men and women together when I was with family or went to my friends' houses. That is all I saw on T.V. The only image I saw from my father, brothers, cousins, and other people was relationships with the opposite sex. I knew the right thing to do and what my heart wanted, but my mind was wondering, why me? Why would a man ever decide to touch a young boy? I started having relations with girls and women.

In my mind, to convince or make sure I only desired females, I had sexual encounters with a lot of women. I never was into girls my age nor younger. After years of the mental battle, I had in my head, I was okay, and those thoughts left my head. Most men who have been touched felt abandoned by his mother, grandmother, or mother figure and has an internal battle within themselves. Those actions will shape his views towards women and, eventually, how he treats women. For me, I viewed situations with women as I going to get mine (sex) and be her to the decision of walking out my life.

During my freshman year in high school, I meet this senior, she was cool, and for some reason, I started seeing her more and more. I will call her Wild Child. We would talk in the hallways, then it went to phone calls and start coming to the house. My grandmother allowed me to go outside on the patio and chill with her. We would just talk and enjoy the nightly breeze. Just good conversation, which eventually leads to other things, but you know how those things happen. This was an everyday thing that occurred between us, but I also would see time to time these guys come to the school to see her. I will call them Beavis and Butt-Head.

After observing them coming to the school, I notice Beavis was the lead, and Butthead just rode in the car, you know, he the tail of the crew and leads nothing, just a follower. This Beavis was her dude, and I was shocked. Wild Child has a dude; why would she be talking to me? But, hey, I am a freshman, and it is not my girl, so I am cool. I had a few run-ins with Beavis and Butthead, but it was cool; he soon found out I was not that dude to be playing with. He tried to come to the hood and make a few plays, I shut that down quick.

Furthermore, I am just here to have fun with Wild Child. She, not my girl. The situation between us moved forward, and we had some good times together. Our families knew each other's, so that made things flow smoothly.

After football games, she would come to pick me up, and we would hang out for a few or whatever we wanted to do. But other situations came up, and I just could clearly see, girls just could not stay true to one guy. I do not know the reason we stop talking or whatever but we still cool; I have not heard nor seen Wild Child in years; she good people. No hard feelings. Life goes on.

I can recall back in 1994, my sophomore year in high school, I meet this freshman female, her name is County Slow at Mississippi State University, my friend was seeing her sister, and he hooked me up. We kicked it, and everything was cool. Well, that is what I thought, but soon did I find out just like a lot of women I had seen in my days. County Slow could not keep her legs close to other men.

I am driving on campus going nowhere in particular, and boom, I saw County Girl coming out the dorm walking across the street with another guy. I just stopped and watched her walk directly in front of my dad's car. She was so lost in the moment, County Girl never looked up nor seen me. I did not blow the horn or get out of the car. That was not my style. I made a few more blocks around campus, seeing what I could see, I did not score, so I drove back home and just chilled.

Later that night, the house phone is ringing, *Hello* I said, "*Hey William,*" she replied. *What is going on?* I asked her, "*oh nothing; just woke up. I had been studying for some tests.*" *Wow, what subjects you got your test on?* She started to lie back-to-back to back. I said dang, it is like the Chicago Bulls with a 3-peat championship run. The lies keep pouring out of her mouth. So, I decided to stop County Slow from continuing to waste her time lying to me, and I told her I knew she was lying and what she was doing with her time. County Girl's action only conformed to me once again that being faithful is not something girls believed in. I have seen this picture before. She was slow and I was just giving her the benefit of the doubt. But since she played herself.

Okay, let the games begin, so after this incident, I started my journey of seeing multiply women at the same time. It was cool. It felt better than sitting around being faithful and knowing that it is a 99.9% chance the woman you thinking your main girl is sleeping with other guys. In the next few years, we spent a lot of time making a lot of great memories together, but I never trusted her again. I was playing the same game. I was playing harder, longer, and stronger. I did not care about anything; she was doing from that point on.

We still played the girlfriend-boyfriend thing, but we both just were cheating and using each other in some way. In 1997, I got another woman pregnant. I had started seeing her after my supposed girlfriend cheated. I had been after this woman for about 2 years or so. I can remember, she walked into the barbershop, I had my 1973 Delta 88, the cleanest ol' Skool car on the streets. I was rolling. It was a Thursday evening; I pulled up to the shop and people everywhere.

I bust in the door, I scan the shop, walk the shop the scope the scene. She was back there, getting her nails done. I told the nail tech, I got her, no problem. I sit down in my brother's barber chair. Ms. Lady is walking out the door, I jumped up, *fool; what you doing?* That my brother talking. *Hold up*, I yelled up once I exited the door. *What is your number?* "Who? Me?" *Yes, you stop playing.* I got the digitals and headed back to the barbershop. Man, if I only knew what the world of hell, I just got myself into.

I thought I was doing it big. I got woman 10 years older than me; I am changing the game. *This is the crap*; I was telling myself. In my mind, I do not see none of my peers making moves like this. Like the old saying goes, if I knew back then, what I know now. This decision to deal with her changed my life forever. I do not look back on it as a negative situation; I appreciate those times because it helped develop me.

That experience is giving me a chance now to provide you with insight into specific actions that can derail your life for years to come. So, let me dive into that life-changing movement for a few moments. As I stated earlier, I got the phone number, and I did not call, and I totally forgot about her until one Thursday night.

Black Knight and I were headed back from Jackson, Mississippi, handling business. Back in the 1990's the only way to get to and from Starkville to Jackson, Mississippi, you had to travel down old Hwy.25. We were rolling listen to rap music, and it hit my mind, I need to holler at Ms. Lady. I knew where she stayed because I been there before. I played football and hung out from time to time with her nephews. I jump out, and she answered the door; we talk and made plans from there. This was the beginning part of me understanding how deep this game is played.

Once again, its repetitive cycle, Ms. Lady got a man. This is a funny scenario of specific revealing to her relationship; she had to go on. I never in my life provide you with such a thing, and to this day, I never ran across it again personally or through a story being told to me. Her actions never spoke or showed, I have a boyfriend. If County Slow was not at my house, Ms. Lady was. Back in those days, I never asked a woman if she had a mate. It was never my concern; I had already envisioned a woman as a cheating woman, so no big deal. My head was still so big currently walking around school and just the town. Furthermore, the most giant demon in my life was brewing inside of me.

The daily sex was I had with these two ladies, especially Ms. Lady, was turning me into a sex addict. I can recall having sex several times a day, before school, lunch break, after school, and throughout the night as I was supposed to be sleeping for school. I was only sixteen at this point in my life. I carried this addiction with me for almost 20 more years and remember in my mind, I had to make sure the demons of my molestation were not going to be a problem. But I was sure I had no desire to ever be with a man. My mind was solely on women, and I wanted them all.

Back to the discovery of Ms. Lady having a man, it was a Thursday night, I was at her place, and one of her friends was there as well. We were just chilling and talking, *"oh dang,"* she said and jumped up. "I *got to go get this man and take him to get some lunch."* Okay, just drop me off and I am cool. *"No,"* she replied, *"I do not have time for that."* Yes, you do, I do not get into those games. The game is about to change for me. Ms. Lady said, *"Waldo is going to give me all his check, and if you ride down there with me, I will give you $250 and every two weeks after that."*

So, why we stay sitting here? That was my question to them. We (me, Ms. Lady, and her friend) riding to his job, Waldo is waiting outside; I opened the door to get in the back; n*o*, she said, *"he will get in the back."* To myself, I am saying, *I know darn well no one in the world is that slow.* But, hey Waldo is, and he got in the back. I spoke, you know my folks always told me to talk to people and be polite.

"What you want to eat;" Ms. Lady asked Waldo? *I want some,* *"McDonald's and go cash my check."* I am sitting on the passenger side of her car, dying laughing and just shaking my head. I can only say to myself, man, *it is some cold-hearted women in this world. But, oh well, better him than me. Let us get this over with, and I can go home.* Now, back at Waldo's job, they get out and he hands on the money. Ms. Lady just walks away and he just looking. His mind, body, and soul must be speaking to him. They just got me.

Ms. Lady's walls back to the car, get in, and hand me 250 dollars. I know she is not going anywhere. For the next several months, every other Thursday, I received my $250 payment plus other gifts and things.
All this bad behavior went on for a long time, and it was a deadly game to be playing for both of us. Ms. Lady was taking this man hard earning money and I was accepting it and spending it, I got it.

I would not advise this for anyone who is reading this book. I was young, dumb, and just enjoying life. I did not need his money nor the drama that came with her. This a coldblooded woman; she played so many games with men, her kids, and whoever would go around her. Waldo and I had a few run-ins, but he did not want any problems. As I got older, I got a clear understanding of his distaste for me. I could not blame him.

For years, I dealt with and accepted this behavior in my life. Obviously, I was not forced, no gun put to my head, nor anything where my life was threatened to be a part of these acts. **LET'S REMEMBER FOR REDEMPTION TO HAPPEN IN YOUR**

LIFE, YOU HAVE TO BE ACCOUNTABLE FOR YOUR ACTIONS.

This sexship went on until 2000, but the devilish acts from Ms. Lady did not stop until 2015. I want to be very clear and understand me, it's nothing Ms. Lady did to me before 2000 could compare to the pain, she poured on me, like she did when it came to my offspring. I learned a lot from her; it shaped my insane thinking for many years forward—the thought I had towards women. In life, learning different lessons will come from various outlets. I have always viewed any situation as a good learning experience. My life would continue with up and down experiences with different women; I did not engage in any relationships after these incidents. I was just enjoying the moments with other women.

Let us move on to another level in Love.

I need you to pay close attention to this section of love; it will be an eye-opener. This will help you understand how past actions and participation in lousy behavior will help you Sabotage yourself. Okay, lets vibe for a few minutes. It is tricky because the woman or man might show a few bad habits you have seen in the past ladies or men, but an extended overall mind, body, and soul are incomparable. Your growth, real friends, mentor, spiritual leader, or some who can help you identify the difference is very vital to you during these trails.

After playing for so long, you will decide, I am ready to settle down and be blessed with the woman or man of my dreams. To some people, that is a scary move in their lives, and it was the same for me, but I knew I also wanted a wife, kids at home, working, and just enjoying life with my family.

DESPERATION IS THE MOST DANGEROUS PLACE YOU CAN BE IN LIFE BECAUSE YOUR THINKING IS NOT LOCKED IN.

You ready, you have played different games, she has played various games with you. Your life with love has been this rollercoaster from hell. You do not want any part of this ride anymore; I am ready for something tangible and real, something that will be able to stand the rain. You pray about, you dream about it, you can smell, feel, and taste this love. You identify her, and she identifies you.

Her smile is flawless, her voice is magical, her intelligence and soul bring solace to your life. The day is here, and Sunshine just came into your universe. You cannot wait to talk with her, see her, touch her, and just chill. As time passes alone, she is all that, and what others might say does not truly matter. Sunshine is the lady that moves you in every way possible. She does not know it nor at the junction in the friendship that you are locked in for life.

The beginning is so appealing—you in hog heaven. Everything going well, but your mind is playing tricks with you on the other side of your brain. You say you ready but you, not because you cannot respect, care, love, protect or provide, But the past women have damaged you to the point of return. Then the game gets more profound, you and Sunshine have been talking, and she starts showing you things that are a turnoff. The friendship/relationship you share is not just between the two of the parties involved.

You push forward, and you discuss your issues with her, but she somewhat discredits your feelings and focuses on what makes her comfortable. Sunshine is satisfied with these actions because it is the behavior that has engulf her entire family with these harmful actions. Above all things, Sunshine is totally different than anyone you met and definitely hands down in her family. So, let's ride this one out.

Sunshine and I were like ice and water; we are meant for each other. She was my oil, and I was that 1973 Delta 88; I needed her inspiration, mindset, ambitious demeanor, kiss, hell just everything about her. My behavior, on the other hand, did not speak to that; I was living a total lie. I had another 2-3 lives going on while dating Sunshine.

Am I doing Sunshine the same way the other women were doing me? Just another reminder this book is about being real, open, honest about the events in my life, and being accountable for such actions. Yes, I was doing the same stuff to a degree. I would be faithful for a while, and if I thought she did or knew she did anything to dishonor me, I would go back to the world I was comfortable in. The women were nothing to me just a day at the park playing pickup basketball.

I had no desires for any other woman, but Sunshine and what was so silly about me. I did not display those feelings 100% of the time. At times, I would act totally different than I felt inside, and I was protecting myself from a woman who only deeply in her heart wanted the best for both of us and the kids. I had let her down so much it is like I just keep running from her and doing foolish things.

I was doing things; she was doing something, and I am not saying she was cheating on me. I would never put her in that category like the other women, but Sunshine did things I did not like. She crossed the line in many ways, but something always drew me back to her and vice versa. We continue to rock and roll together, but the demons inside of me took over. I was able to forgive, but not forget the actions. I continue to hear conversations about our relationship which no one else should have known. Sunshine just would not stop dishonoring our relationship; instead, she put her outside the family in our family's business.

I will continue to do what I do. I ran the checks up and women. It is what I know how to do. It is like 1+1=2, I cannot get the problem wrong, and I cannot lose. It is a beautiful life. It was great; that is the lie I was telling myself and everyone else who would ask me. I was cold and I felt I was free, but I was the biggest dummy walking around on earth. I was allowing small gossip crap to destroy us and anything we tried to build together. You can refer to the beginning of the section, I said this was going to be tricky.

Your mind is playing tricks on you. Oh, Sunshine, just like my mom, she left me, so Sunshine will leave also. No doubt, so why care? Wild Child, Country Slow, Ms. Lady and so many others cheated, hell, Sunshine will do the same. I did everything within my power to run Sunshine off and I did. The first time in my life, a woman told me she was leaving. I was broken, I was damaged, I was embarrassed, I was at the lowest point of my life.

I had everything I ever dreamed of My OWN FAMILY, AND I BLOW IT. It was so much going on in the household and I let the situation get out of hand. My disrespect level for our kids and I was at an all-time high. I was not the man, I was not the top provider, protect, comforter, listener, and on top of that, I was a habitual liar, cheater, verbal abuser, and just a nobody for my actions. I was depressed.

My self-esteem was at rock bottom. I was not active, nothing in the household. I was just there, and she is standing strong fighting for the family, and I am doing everything in my power to destroy it. I went out and made several business deals that loaded my pocket with money, but those arrangements were something a man should not do. I was making deals with another woman. Yes, money is needed and depending on your situation and lifestyle, you going to need a ton of it.

But remember, **MONEY IS THE ROOT OF ALL EVIL. If YOU DO NOT HANDLE IT RIGHT. NEVER LOSE YOUR**

INTEGRITY NOR DIGNITY, BECAUSE OF MONEY OR HOW YOU GET IT.

I did so much over the years, and I will need another book to give details from start to finish. As men and women, we sometimes put ourselves in a situation that is not true. We have a self-basis view on life, and it can be very detrimental to our health, families, and just livelihood in general.

HOW TO REDEEM LOVE?

I had many challenges in my life. And most of my challenges were simple. I made this adjustment and boom; I am back rolling. But this section of my life was the most prominent mountain I had to climb and too be truthful, I am still got my spikes on.

First, you must identify the problem, and for a lot of people, it will stop right there. Why? Because people do not like to get naked in the mirror and talk about the negatives things they have done. It is hard, I will admit it, and I can recall when I was left standing all alone. It was raining, it was pouring down, and I just got out of the shower. I walked over to the mirror and wiped away the steam. As I am wiping, I can see this broken and lost soul. So, after the senseless pity party, I asked God *what happened to me*? My son, He replied, it is time to be honest and real with yourself. I submerged myself into the wrongs I was doing. I will repeat, **I SUBMERGED MYSELF INTO THE WRONGS, I DONE.**

I did not look at her faults, I did not start ranting about she did this, nor she did that. Neither did I think about what others did to me. It was my fault because I allowed specific behavior around me, and I engulfed myself in such actions as well.

I focused only on my actions and my toxic behaviors. I had to go back into my childhood and figure out where this dysfunctional behavior came from?

Before I go into details of the route I took, you must clearly understand. You can blame, point fingers at mom, dad, siblings, friends, different mates you had, or a dog. It will not matter, and it will not help you fix what is wrong with you. Your redemption story is about you, period. You cannot become a better man or woman if you are stuck on blaming someone else besides yourself. You the problem; how in the world, you think, you can fix another adult. Your happiness or future happiness lies within you not them. You cannot fix other people period. You will continue to be on a merry go round.

Therefore, I went back to the past, and I realize I started into this life of girls too early. Okay, I cannot do anything about that, so let us take that out of the equations. My mother left me, okay, why my mother did not want me? I was not good enough to be raised with my other siblings. Okay, I asked before and never received an answer. I can remove that portion of the problem. Why? My actions towards any woman I dealt with had nothing to do with a decision my parents made about my living situation.

I used my mother not being in my life as my own excuse for lackluster behavior. It was an easy way of not being accountable for my actions. So, who are you blaming for still acting in a boyish or girlish manner? You classify yourself as a man or a woman, right? It is time to set up and do what you need to do as an adult. It is get going time. You cannot continue to be bullied by your own behavior. It is time to get up and fight for your relationship or get prepared to be in the relationship you always wanted.

Nancy G. Robinson, my grandmother, and Ms. Marlene Simpson, my stepmother taught me, how to carry myself. Plus, I saw how some men treated their lady. I showed no consistency in my situations. I noticed what a provider, protector, and all the things that come with being a man entitles. The main thing my grandmother and Aunt Betty always said to me, **TREAT PEOPLE HOW YOU WANT TO BE TREATED.**

The enemy in your head will trick us into believing you cannot do this; you will not ever be that other person inside of you. You will always be that messed up adult who came from a jacked-up environment. But truth be told, if you ever discover what the enemy already saw inside of you, they know you are unstoppable. After, I looked myself in the mirror and took accountability for my own actions. I went to work, I started to exercise, eat better, read about relationships, scriptures about Love and Respect. I began to see a counselor.

My counselor opened my mind on dealing with past issues, so they can be burned and washed away. We also discussed my sex addiction; I was dealing with daily. And I was able to gain the necessary tools to handle my decades-long problem with sex. I did not respect myself; my self-esteem was trash.

Sex was my coverup; it kept me from handling specific problems. Like a drug, it was my escape from reality. Sex had once again taken over my life. Sex was more important than anything or anyone. I am just being real with you and trying to help you. My addiction to sex probably not your fix but food, drama, lying, stealing, being a physical or verbal abuser, or whatever it is. But whatever your addiction is, seek help as soon as possible.

I am asking you do not let whatever your personal issue ruins your life and the people in your life. Seek help aggressively and do not stop until you found the right person you can vibe with. On this redemption journey of love, you going to have to put yourself second at times or even further than that on the pole. I need you to focus not on selfishness but being selfless. It is a totally different ball game when you change from being selfish to selfless.

When one is selfish, it is all about them, but when you become selfless, you are motivated with no concern about oneself but for your mate. The transformation is challenging, I won't lie to you, I am still working daily on being selfless and my sex addiction. It is a second by second, minute by minute, hour by hour, day by day, week by week, month by month, and year by year process. It has been the biggest battle of my life. But I am built for this challenge and experience, so I will not lose anymore.

I started to listen to how people feel. I work daily on communication and make sure; I listen to understand and not hear to reply. I continue to work on myself with the wording of the things I say. If you have a terrible relationship, a lot of it can relate back to communication. You will learn everything is not meant for a reply. In a lot of cases, your mate needs your ear, not your mouth. I had learned to be slick at listening and not slick at talking because no one in this world can out-talk me.

To be honest, we give our opinion on a lot of things that truly have nothing to do with our own life. So, why even comment. They do not care about your thoughts on the situations. If they want your advice, they will ask you but make sure when they ask you. You wait a minute and ask first; do you want my advice? If they reply and say yes, then it is your time to go in. Also, it will be helpful if you take a love language assessment. This assessment will genuinely give you insight into your partner's real thoughts and feelings towards certain situations.

This is all comes back to respect, communication, and understanding of your mate. It is selfless. Furthermore, you will trip up and make mistakes. For example, you will say something wrong, you will not be attentive as you should, you will probably yell etc. Some days will be better than other days; we are human, so do not get down on yourself. Life is not about being perfect because that is a free fall.

What is your Some Day? When I say Some Day. I am speaking about, someday (this day) I will take my mate out for dinner; I will pour myself into her/him this day, I will make sure I call them at this time every day, and I will send or take her flowers.

Someday, I will have a great relationship/marriage. Someday I will be a fantastic communicator. Write this day and post it on your mirror. What is going someday? This is a lifelong transformation that you will have to work on daily. I worked on things every day, and it is hard. You cannot get discouraged because your mate is not going to believe your words anymore. IT IS ALL ABOUT ACTIONS.

Here are the steps you will need to take for REDEMPTION to happen in your love life.

1. Stop lying!
2. Honesty and Accountability
3. Communication
4. Action
5. Be a man or woman of your word
6. Last but most importantly SELF LOVE AND WORTH

Chapter 4: What is The Redemption of the Parent?

This book is getting deep, and it will help you refocus your life. I am about to touch on a subject that is real for a lot of men. This chapter is about you and your offspring(s). I know some of you, like myself been through a lot dealing with kids. But as I always say, we will make it past this and being our walk towards redemption with our kids.

It is not a blueprint when talking about being a father. It is no handout when it comes to being a father. Yes, people, your parents, friends, family members, and people in the stores will tell you how to parent your child, but they do not know to be honest. Everyone is giving advice on what works for them, and most of the advice was given to them. We all as parents have said, mommy and daddy said to do it this way or that way. You need to take some of their advice but at the end of the day, you and the mother of the child need to do what is best for the child. **I REPEAT WHAT IS BEST FOR THE CHILD. NOT WHAT IS BEST FOR THE PARENT.**

I became a father before; I was grown. Yes, my age stated, I was an adult, but my mind and actions did not say the same. I was 19 years of age and still chest-deep in the streets. And remember I told you, Ms. Lady and I was having fun. The fun has turned into something else now, and she thought she was locked in for life. It is crazy how some people believe a child is their ticket to a better life. I did not show up to the delivery of my child, and I heard she was so beautiful. My baby looked so much like her grandfather; it was amazing and such an incredible feeling for me. The first two years of fatherhood were cool, strange, nonetheless cool. I had no idea the drama that lied, hiding for my daughter, the countless phone numbers, police being called, and so much more, I would endure for the next 16 years.

Yes, you say to yourself; why you did not take her to court. I thought I allowed my street life to stop me, and I had no desire to be in courtrooms. I was seeing them enough already. No excuse for not stepping up, but just letting you know my mindset at that time. I was so overjoyed to have a daughter, my child, and her mom and brother were at my place, and it was okay. I was doing my thing, working, and hustling, but the tarradiddles and cheating from her never stopped—the leaving in and out with my child. The back and forth was something I never saw before.

So, I made the decision, Ms. Lady needed to leave and go back to her spot. Let the real games beginning. Ms. Lady's goal from that day forward was to torture me, my daughter, and my family. As a father, I just say a lot of dumb mess to see my child. If I would have sex with her and give her money, I had no problems, if my dad gave her money, they had no issues, and the list goes on. It was never about our child; it was all about Ms. Lady in her mind.

I did not know it because I never saw that from my parents. Yes, I was raised at my grandmother's house, but my father never talks down about my mother. I was not from that world, where parents bad-mouthing each other. I do not believe in it and never will go that route.

Ms. Lady saw our daughter as a bag, the money bag, not as I have this beautiful, intelligent, talented child, who would be loved by her mother's side of the family and father's side of the family. Ms. Lady did not have work on her mind, and her focus was controlling us with the baby. When she figured, I cannot control them, so let me make their life a living hell every day.

I can recall this behavior for going on for months and years; over and over; when is it going to stop? I had cried out, a good, long cry, and when much weeping became a dulled edge of my discomfiture, I began to reflect that all was not lost yet. I picked myself up and continue to go over and try to see my child. And, I never knew, Ms. Lady had a deadlier plan. She worked to brainwash our child; this was the next level of the game. My child is kaput.

For the next decade, she made sure our child thought we cared nothing about her. All those years, I tried and tried, but I did not try hard enough. I valued the street life and taking chances with my freedom more, instead of working at the funeral home consistently. I was wrapped up in getting some money than sitting down every opportunity I had and spending it with my daughter. I used the streets to cover my pain. I was decapitating myself and my daughter in a sense. I really was no better than her mother.

The Word states, NO SIN IS GREATER THAN THE OTHER. Yes, I never participated in the brainwashing to convince our child; her mother was this terrible person. I could have, but I always viewed things as; our daughter will discover this activity on her own. But I did other things to help hurt my child's development by taking dangerous trips, in and out of jail dealing with misdemeanor cases. It was crazy.

August of 2004, my first son was born, I got locked up and was fighting a case for most of his mother's pregnancy. I came home almost three months after he was born. In 2005, February 9, to be exact, I took the blow of my life, my hero died, my father, and I was a lost soul for the next 10 years. I was a dead man walking. I finished at the community college and left Mississippi. I went and never returned but for a few months. My life now is over the phone, check in the mail, and road trips to see my kids. I do not know the definition for it, but it is not parenting to me.

I did it, and that was damaging to the kids as well. I moved to a new state, 2 kids, they were born on the same day, and by the same two women, I was seeing back in the day. My son's mother left me in mid-2000, years of excellent and bad times, I did not want to leave the streets. She could not take me living that way. This was after I lost my eye in some street stuff. But hey, it is what it is.

I got to keep moving. We stayed in touch for the next few years. One Sunday afternoon, she called me and said she wanted to see me. Okay, I am down my dad's crib but come through; he would like to see you. She and my father had a cool relationship, but he did not care about no crap; I had it going on with a woman anyway. She came, and I was shocked but hey, who would not want to see me always? I was still the man. We made plans for the following weekend and that was the weekend our son was conceived.

Wow, I got a son now, and I just must keep it real. I was so lost; I did not know; I had anyone in this world. I moved after graduation and never looked back. A few months after, I left Katrina hit New Orleans, and I ended there working. I was there for almost 2 years and boom, probate court dealing with my dad's death and his property. I will not get into those clowns, who played the background, but I am grateful for the experience; I learned a lot.

I am living in the deeper south now; I am living in the sunny state. Man, I was so lost and hopeless, I had no business here. I knew that around 2 months after, I left, but I cannot go back to Mississippi. Damn, I have another child on the way; hold on; this not part of the plan.

Oh well, I will not get into the third child's mother; I have to go back to the second one first. My son's mother and I never had any significant issues about co-parenting. I am joking with you. At the beginning of this journey, things were calm. She was just a typical mom with her first child, she just spoiled, and that was her angel baby. Her words, not mine. We had no issues and no underline evil agendas from her part. The biggest problems we always had and to this day are Communication and making her husband feel comfortable in his position.

I do not believe a man should ever need that justification when it comes to being a father or father figure. I am a straight shooter, and she plays a word game. Or she gets in the mood of you not here crap. It would be times; I would not know for days or weeks if something had happened in my son's life. She would come with her biases to make her feel right about the lack of communication. But it was a point her guy knew, yes it messed with me a lot. I would fall back at times because I am not the things as hit the fan, and I need you to help figure it out father. In other cases, I do not need to know. As I look back on the situation, she was doing what she had to do to keep her marriage and made her comfortable. Do I respect that, hell no, she must answer God on her actions?

I was the absent father; I stated early it is no possible; you can indeed be father hours and miles away. I had no issues every seeing my son. She has done a great job compared to the first woman. If I am going to make that comparison, my son's mother needs to be awarded a Nobel Peace Prize compared to my daughter's mom. However, her decision to play this soft roll and having a soft husband has led to my son thinking certain things in life is cool, and I see those same things the total opposite.

I will move on to the daughter's mother, and to be honest, I knew two months after she was pregnant. I had seen this picture before and this going to be a long and funky ride. I think it was about 2 months in the pregnancy I left Monroe, La and I went to New Orleans for work. It was so much of money been thrown around I had to get it. This was my first job ever in life. I always worked my father's funeral home, but getting direction from someone else, no, this was my first rodeo. I am in New Orleans. It was crazy to see firsthand how this hurricane ripped this city apart. It was like being in a movie; cars abandoned, building damaged, boats on fences, and dead bodies in cars.

The west bank is over the bridge from New Orleans. The drive is only 5-10 minutes, and I was living in Gretna, La. I think 30 of us went down there to work. I was not in contact with no one. My best friend Sleepy, my brother B, my sisters Pam and Angie, my uncle Jessie, my cousin/little brother Blair are the only people I told, I was moving and that's who I barely communicated with during these dark days. My life is so out of control, I had no one I knew I could talk with about anything in my life. So, we here to work, we are sleeping in tents, and it is always some movement. I would just lay in my tent with my firearm under my sleeping bag and just cry and pray, pray, and cry. I had nothing else, no fight in me. I was lost. I was lost. I was so grateful my kids' mothers were taking care of them because I was in no place to do anything for my kids. I am talking emotionally nor physically.

I get a call from my brother Bailey; I got to come home and handle some business. I go see my Uncle Jessie; I did not know that would be my last time seeing him alive. A few weeks later, my little brother Blair calling saying he is dead. One the last few men who stuck with me before, during, and after my father's death is gone now.

The hole is getting more in-depth, and I do not know what to do but to keep fighting and trying to do something with my life. I would like for you to pause for a few minutes. And picture yourself on an island alone, no one around you is familiar. You just lost your father, who never left your side, your uncle who was helping you heal is gone, the relationship is nothing with your daughter and son is too young to even know what is going on in life. The relationship is nothing with your mother.

The memorial service for your uncle comes around, and I go home and attend the service. I remember I was in Starkville, Mississippi, trying to comfort others and I am dead inside. I was able to reunite with my people from California. This October of 2005 and I was able to meet a special friend. It was crazy; she was the help I needed at this moment.

I roll back to Louisiana and back to the grind. I worked a few days, and I was like, let me go home to surprise her. One of the worse decisions I made, and I found out she was smoking cigarettes and pregnant with my child.

I wanted to kill her on sight. I told her I was done; I left and drove back to work. After this incident, I never viewed her the same. How can any woman, especially a woman of her age and underline health issue, jeopardize her baby?

I phoned my sister Angie; I cannot do this, explaining the situation, and she informed me, you cannot walk away now. You must wait after the child is born and move from there, Okay cool. Deadly, one called and did everything to explain away her actions. But her words meant nothing, and I informed her, you are free to do whatever and see whomever because I will be doing the same.

What is wrong with me? I was sick and messed up in the head. I keep making these stupid childish decisions. So, we waited for the birth of our child. I took a break from work and went to the house for a few days. I was on the toilet, and she walks in, water coming down her leg. I did not know what was going on. *Deadly One are you pissing on yourself?* "No, William, my water broke," *oh dang,* so we rolled to the hospital. I stayed there with her until her family arrived, and I headed back to work. She stayed there until my second daughter was born. I received a call, and the doctor stated he would have to deliver the baby early. Back on the road again, my baby was two pounds and nine ounces. This cannot be real. My daughter was born two and a half months early, I was devasted. Yes, I questioned God, yes, I was broken, and yes, I wanted to hurt Deadly One.

I made it back to town, and my child is in NICU inside this incubator with tubes everywhere. I could not stop crying inside, I could not look at my child this way, and I had no conversation for her mother. I sat around for a few days and consulted with the doctor about her uphill battle. I went back to work; I got to keep moving. If I sit around the hospital or just at home, I would have lost it. I would work for a few days and come back for a few days.

My daughter had to get blood transfusions, hair shaved off, IV in her head, arms, and anywhere they could place them. It was horrifying. I did not know what to do, so I just talked and formed a bond with the doctors and nurses. They were so lovely and helpful throughout the process. The focus is shifted for me, and all of everything was about my kids not having a relationship. We had nothing left, and to be honest, it was nothing there in the beginning. I tried to take a friendship and turn it into a lifelong commitment. But I shook off the bad feeling I had towards her.

Our child needs us, so we did our best to work together. The co-parenting relationship was cool, with no problems; we had one common goal and a great understanding of the purpose.

We went our separate ways, and I was upset about the situation and how I handled it. I was cool; we were cool with the communication and everything that had to do with raising a child together. It worked well for the next 4-5 years.

Our child was getting better daily, and I had moved to Saint Louis, Mo. On the road again and the main point, I am further away from all my kids. The journey of the road bandit began. Every two months, I rent a car and make my journey to Georgia to Mississippi and spend time with the kids and head back to STL.

I lived in Saint Louis for 8 months and headed to Big D, Dallas, Texas. At that moment, it was the best move I could have made in my life and my kids' life. My stay in Missouri was beautiful; it helped me grow up in a lot of ways. I was ready for the game-changer, and Dallas was that for my life. I made a move and back to the regular routine; every two months, I rent a car and head to Georgia to Mississippi and spend time with my kids. Things were becoming familiar while in Dallas for me. I moved to Arlington from Pleasant Grove, and the game had escalated. My life is going cool, and I finally was done with the probate court.

That was 5 years of drama, which I wanted no part of it and one of the best decisions I made in my life. Let us get back to Deadly One, she took a blow to her life, and I had empathy for her because I saw a parent start going into their last stage of life. She did not have the tools needed to handle the knowing my mom is going to die any day. And honestly, a lot of people do not know how to seize and take back control of their life. I felt her pain, and I do not wish the experiment of losing a close parent on anyone. If a person is not built for it, it is a high possibility you lose your mind. Her mother was an outstanding and loving woman.

I have the utmost respect for her. The times we spent together, she was about educating you, respecting you, and showing you the most love she could give you. This event leads to a downward spiral for Deadly One's life. I completely understood. I tried my best to support in any form but getting back together was her idea of me helping, and I was not ever going to back.

The situation got worse, and I had to go get my baby. I was scared as hell, so I arrived in Georgia and seeing her and our child in that living condition blew my mind. This was Deadly One, regardless of our personal relationship and her decision during the pregnancy. I knew she did not live this way, but I also knew I had to do what was best for our child.

I got our daughter and headed back to Texas with a 2-year-old and had no clue about raising a girl. I had some help from someone else, which was a great relief. I just did what I knew to do, but the girly stuff, I turned that over to my friend girl to handle. She was terrific with my child, and I still could not thank her enough for all she did for my daughter.

As a father, I did the best I could with the knowledge I had. The decision I made to get our daughter while she healed turned our co-parenting relationship into a devilish battle from her side. Deadly One could not grasp the thought of a man, being a man, and raising a child. My view was totally different, and I did what any father would do. But I learned everyone does not think logically.

Her thoughts where I am the enemy now, and she was going to do anything in her power to destroy me and anything I tried to do in life. Deadly One would talk to anyone I had a relationship with and tell some of the most ridiculous tarradiddles. I would hear about Deadly One's statements, and some would believe them, repeat them to try to belittle my character.

I knew then those people were just as ignorant as she was. In life, people try to get in the information they can about you to use as a weapon. No weapon formed against me shall prosper. While I lived in Dallas, I met my baby boy's mother. We went from 0 to 100 first, but it was a great feel. She lived in a different area. But we bonded fast, and it was magical at first. I was back to me, and I was ready for a family.

I was ready in my mind, but not my heart. Your mind can say one thing, but your heart/passion can be on separate pages. She is cool people, crazy, not literary, so do not get it twisted. She gave birth to My Hero and My Buddy. Red is about business and about what is best for the child, period. I have no complaints about how she went about the pregnancy and her no games mindset. I could not ask for anything better if I had to compare it to the previous experience. And to be honest, I only had one of my kids' mother that thought taking any type of chance would be okay.

The miscommunication Red and I had on a personal level did not usually cross over into the co-parentship. The relationship as parents was solid. I was there in the delivery room when our son was born. I loved experience, I never been in that situation, and I played a significant role in helping her.

She got nervous, and I had to come to change the mood in the room, so she could focus and handle that business. It was a delightful scene. I was zoned in as a father, and my whole purpose was to be a better father. I had prayed, fought hard to control my demons, but again I failed.

The issue about the co-parenting with Red is she will get upset about something I did to her personal. And, if I called for my son and it's no answers for days. The common excuse, I forgot to call back or whatever crap she could think to tell me. To be honest, she had issues before in previous situations, and she did not want to repeat it with our son. If you ask her, she will tell my leaving and coming in and out of the house caused issues within the home.

My inconsistency was a killer to our son. I showed some crazy behaviors around our son, such as verbal abuse, outrages cussing, one day I would be there, and if too much drama continued between us personally, I would leave and did not think I was wrong.

I will give Red credit for not going as far as some of my other kids' mothers. After she would get out her personal feelings and recognize it not about her, things will return to normal. I did not have to worry about the safety of our child. Red was always there and had saved our child a few times.

HOW A FATHER REDEEMS HIMSELF?

Fear is deadly, you can be paralyzed by fear and incapable of thinking clearly, proper dialogue, and the list goes on. I was afraid before when it came to taking my kids' mother to court about her uncontrollable desire to keep me away from our child. I allowed my street life to keep me from filing paperwork. Plus, I never thought a judge who cares less about our child nor us should decide. But fellows, whatever you are doing, stop it and take her to court if necessary.

You must show your kids, daddy is trying everything within his power to be in your life. The court fee is little money to get you a date in court. As a father, you have equal rights as the mother has to the kid.

The war will be long, but you can make it to the finish line. Also, show up to your kids' events and show them you care because the mother is telling them a different story. Furthermore, I know a lot of men who decided to stop seeing their child because the personal relationship was over. If you one of those men. You need to man-up and apologize to both. And rebuild your relationship with your child. Fathers, I know you're saying, hold on homie; what about the woman who made it difficult for me?

I understand fellows, I have been to hell and back with my two girls' mothers. We cannot control another person's actions. We must pray and continue to fight for our kids. I do not recommend you get into the battle; of who is the better parent with your child?

God will see you through the process. And one day, you will have the opportunity to tell your Truth. That battle will be an endless cycle and a waste of time. You will have a better outcome of just taking her to court. I remember going through my redemption process with my kids; I just was honest with them and allowed them to ask me any questions. I was open, honest, and I did not get into the point of making their moms look bad.

At the end of the day, their mom is still their mom and vice versa. I made a point of talking with my kids daily, going to support them, and I even lost jobs to make sure I was there. Have I done everything right? No, that's an impossible task. Most of all, forgive yourself and start from that day. You, as a father, will have to be rhythmic in this process. This will be a slow and tidies journey. You cannot think the change will be immediately nor go the way you feel it should go.

Remember, you are dealing with another individual and a child who has been stressed and depressed about their parents' lack of adultness. As men, we are leaders, so we need to lead the way. I took a lot of punches; I been lied on by previous kids 'mother to the other one. And some are so eager to hear anything negative they will believe it. They will repeat it to you, their fake family, and friends, but that is not your issue. That is fine as well, you know, what your characteristics are built on.

I am giving you insight on different scenarios to be on the lookout for. Stand Tall. Redeeming yourself does not mean I will allow this person to treat me like nothing. The focus and only focus are the kids.

The steps you will need to take for REDEMPTION to happen in your parenting life

1. Be accountable; you helped plant the seed.
2. Remove your personal feelings from the equations
3. Honesty with your child
4. Be there, be fearful
5. Love conquers all

Father are vital to their kids upbring. The encouragement and insight our children need will take them far in life. We can expect our kids to go out in the world and be successful, if we are damaging them at home. Remember kids are like bank account, they only get out what we put in them. In life different situation will happen, but we must stand the course with our children.

I need you to clearly understand our kids study us, just like we study them. The level of communication is so important within the relationship with your child. As a parent, you must adapt and adjust for the betterment of the child. Also be aware of your kids' actions and if they trying to play parents against each other. This behavior must be addressed head on. The co-parent relationship must be solid and as parents, we have to stop worrying about, who is actually controlling or as I call it winning in the situation.

Most importantly is the kid winning. Is the kid winning in life? Does your child feel he or she is caught in the middle of you'll crap?

Bert Robinson

Chapter 5: What is Your Redemption Story?

Redemption is played on different stages for each individual person. Heavy lassitude settled upon me as I walked away from my past life. There had been too much enjoyment (genuine excitement and some a lot of smokescreens) in my past 27 years of life. The smokescreens were all about hiding the hurt, pain, abandonment, and confusion I was dealing with in life.

I used different situations and made a lot of bogus decisions that put me in the hole. I know I created those holes, and I am not here to place nor sound like others are the blame. Why would you say you might be asking yourself?

I allowed myself to make the final choices to sell drugs, run the streets, deal with those women, move from Starkville, put my kids in a situation of not seeing me daily, not taking those mothers to court, and so on. I could have gone to school, dived headfirst in the funeral business, work harder to be the best talent on the football, basketball, or baseball field.

But the other phony life was more important to me. I said phony because at the end of the day, if you not living a righteous lifestyle, you are phony. A lot of people play different phony life games, but that is fine and all as well. People will die and live-in misery to enjoy their self-bias lifestyle.

A self-bias lifestyle is a life that is a person that always takes credit for anything positive that contributes to their life or anyone's life that involved them. But on the flip side, they will always blame others for anything negative. Those the people when you on your redemption tour in life, you must separate yourself. It could be your wife, husband, sister, brother, best friend, and eventually could be your own child.

For example, A wife is pleased with the direction her marriage is going, and she tells herself and personal circle, she is doing such a great as a wife. But when obstacles hit the marriage, *my husband is not a good partner,* and points at all his mishaps and keeps her dirt to herself.

A child is successful in school and sports, a single mother will take credit for all her hard work to make it possible for the child. When the same child fails at certain things, it becomes the father's lack of whatever that caused the child to fail. You must determine as a man or woman to decide what is your righteous life to live. I had figured out a long time ago. I just was not fully ready to stop playing with my life. I was comfortable swimming in the dirty waters of my ways.

I was comfortable, and you might be comfortable as well, but at what price are you willing to pay. Is your kids' life worth it? Are you willing to have your kids continue the cycle of dysfunctional behaviors? Let us be real, you saw your mom or dad do the same stuff that you're currently doing to your kids.

Some areas in our lives do not have to be part of our redemption story. We can stop and change the course at any moment. Or you can be like me; see the problem, identified it, and still decide to live recklessly. I would not recommend that path. I can be real about it, and I liked the course I took; why because God had already written my story. God knew I would waste hundreds of thousands of dollars. He knew I would be a cheater. God knew I was going to leave my kids and move away, He knew I was going to be everything, and God knew I would have a redemption story that would rock the world and help change millions of lives.

It does not matter your age, gender, race, religion, or living condition. You can start on your pathway today, and I encourage you to look within your soul. You have no clue that your story can be that one to save a life. I was told so many years ago, *you have a story Bert,* and you can be that person. I was afraid to face my truths about myself, so once I did it and become comfortable within myself. I was ready to start redeeming myself.

I set out on a mission, and I contacted any person I could, and I apologized for any harmful actions. I was successful in 97% of the cases, but the rest I could not contact, which is okay as well. I tried. My point is to give a sincere and 150% effort in your redemption. This is a redirection of your attitude towards life. When your perspective on life changes, then your performance in life will change as well. I am telling you from experiences, and I hope you get this; do not continue to wait to change, just to add more to your redemption story.

The longer you wait and procrastinate, the deeper your holes get. The earlier you embrace the changes which are necessary for your life, the faster your attitude and lifestyle will be swift in your life and everyone else surrounding you. We are on the redemption tour of our life. Yes, I am giving you nuggets to take with you, but I also understand; this might not be your time to turn it around. I am joking with you.

It is your time right now to stop all the crap and redeem yourself. We are here to win and kill the dysfunctional cycles that have held you and your people in bondage for decades. If you're not feeling me, then you're not grasping how serious this journey is for your life. How about this? Take yourself out of the equation and put in your kids, spouse, or whomever you love in that space. I look at life in quarters, and you can put in the perspective of a football or basketball game.

You're the man/woman on your team, and the whole game, you have been pathetic, dropping passes, overthrowing receivers, bouncing the ball out of bounds, and missing open shots. These actions have been repeating the whole game. You're the leader, and everyone is counting on you, but for some reason, your game is off today.

You keep trying, and you keep failing as well. The coaches, teammates, fans, and your family is counting on you. Hell, you are counting on you, and it seems like there isn't any hope. This regular performance continues to take place for several games, weeks, and you just do not understand. My friend, you are in a significant slump, and no relief is coming soon.

It is the four-quarter now, and you get your first touchdown pass, or your first jumper went in the basketball. Suddenly, the tide has changed, and you on a roll. Pass after pass or bucket after bucket, and the whole game is back in your control. Your family, fans, teammates, and coaches are cheering you on. The man/woman is back, and you have taken control of the situation.

Do you understand that is how life is for some people? Some of the most gifted people, who are classified as celebrities, go through this daily, but do you not get you are a celebrity as well. The kids you helped birthed are looking for you to come out of your slump. Your spouse, your siblings, your friends, and the kid who is looking up to you is patiently waiting for you to turn the game around.

That is one of the elements of redemption. It is not about the hundred times you fail in life, but each time you got up off the ground and continue to fight. People will turn away, tune you out, count you out, and most of the time, start talking about you as if you never were great nor had the talent. They will consider you the biggest bust of the decade. It is Life. Therefore, never get too low nor high on yourself. You must remain humble in the thing call Life.

Everyone one of us has a story about the trials and tribulations in their life. Mine is mine, and yours are yours but let's not keep those bottled up. You know how great it can be to help someone else. I am sure it is some who can be encouraged by your courage to speak openly about your redemption story. You will open yourself for criticism, ok, and do you not understand those same people were talking badly about you anyway. Furthermore, those people are the ones who are closes to you. This is your way of releasing your pain and redeeming yourself.

Redemption: The Next Phase...

I had to redeem myself from being homeless, so I woke up one day and had nowhere to go and no plan, hope, food, or anything besides car and clothes. I used to go around to different places to park my car and fall asleep. At times it was so cold until my body became numb to the coldness. I had no money for food, so I would go to places like Wal-Mart or grocery stories and pretend I was shopping so I could eat.

You know I was not tripping because I was in the situation, I was tripping because no one came to get me. My people could careless was my thoughts and outlook, but why would I be tripping now? It was that way all my life. I am used to being alone and left behind. That's what makes me the warrior I am. That's what drives me so I can redeem myself so my family will understand yes; I am sick in the head; yes, I go into my shell and do not talk nor be around people because I am afraid to get close to people.

More than anything I want you to understand, you not alone in your journey. I want you to understand this book is for all the underdogs, the people who were counted out by everyone. I recall after the summer of 1995; I was kicked out of school for something I was involved in during the summer. So, this is not the fairy tale story people thought. This is some real-life coming out of the mud.

You must be able to reach deep inside of yourself and come out of the hole. Today, everyone wants instants gratification before doing anything in life. This world, as of today, is about participation trophies. Just show up and take a selfie. You got street cred because of the likes and hearts you get on social media. Post a picture of your body, you the woman, take a picture with a tough-looking face and you a gangsta now. It is time to stop the crap and be bold, be open, be the next Redemption story.

You ever had siblings, but you rarely saw them or was around them. It was so bad people did not even know those were your people. I am deeper into my life because I feel I have that person I have not reached yet. A lot of you already judged and put me in a particular category anyway, so your assessment about me is fair. I am totally comfortable with who I am as a man. I know I have issues, and I have never had a problem getting help for my mental issues. I hope you not the type of person to judge a man or woman, and your house is made from glass.

I also pray you to use your testimony to help release someone else from their darkness and not let fear cause you to go into a darker area. I can help you go from surviving to thriving, I have done it, and I am doing it daily. I work 18 hours a day, 5 days a week. I am putting in hours to show God I am worthy of His blessings and calling on my life. You are worthy also; just release yourself and turn your life over to God.

I left my old life, and people I never dreamt of knowing start walking into my life and pouring knowledge on me. God knew I was ready to handle the load, and I was walking in my purpose. You ever lost a vital body part?

Have people ever looked strangely at you because you were different than everyone else in the room? So, you cannot tell me, I do not understand what redemption is about. I hear to let you know; it is possible to trust me. I know how it feels when you have only one person in life to believe in you. I know what it felt like when God sent my best friend/Godfather, Sleepy Robinson, to come to get me out of living in that roach motel and allowed me to change my life when everyone just laughed and talk about me.

I learned about the 3 F's: FAITH, FAMILY, AND FINANCES. He spent days and hours to pour education in me about life. That is the part of the reason I am so strong now. It will always be WBR4L. Sleepy the only person who takes time out to help me with my dying father and taking us every Tuesday to eat frog legs.

That whole experience was a revelation, and it taught me how to be a real man. Yes, I know I let him down also, but I never crossed him nor directly disrespected him. We are too solid for that. Men, I must speak on this because a lot of us play this tough role, and all the time, we are dying inside. We must stop telling ourselves and kids that men do not show emotions. Men, we must stop running from issues that are detrimental to our mental and physical health. I will speak on two topics that are damaging to a lot of men.

Some are men dealing with their father never being around, and you're holding on to that pain. Some men are coping with being touched or molested at a young age and afraid to tell someone or get counseling.

Well, my fellows, I am here for you and will share my own personal stories on both topics, and I hope you get some help from somewhere.

I can help you, as well. I will start with the absent parent; I did not grow up with my mother nor siblings, and some instincts I went months and years not seeing both. As a young boy, I never knew the impact of not having my mother around. I figured my grandmother was the best replacement for me.

Yes, Nancy G. Robinson was the best, but the nurturing, connection, talks, care, love, and insights I should have gathered from my mother I did not happen. I feel like we are strangers around each other; I felt lost and afraid to sit with her alone. I want you to clearly understand and hear me well; my mother is a real woman. She is not a horrible woman, so do not get it twisted. I am speaking about my life experiences and what issues I have within me.

I have spent time with my mom, and the knowledge she has given me as an adult is incredible, but I wish I got it coming up in life. God had a different plan for me and a different purpose in my life. My mother is cool as the other side of the pillow; she is a brilliant woman, and to be honest, still to this day, I have no clue; why I ended up at my grandmother's house. Both of my parents failed in communications about the situation.

Let me get back to the topic. I had moments when I went to my mother's house, but my daily growing-up with her and my sibling stop early in my life. I felt unwanted by my mother, and it was a dark cloud over my life until I turned 37 years old. But by that time, I was ruined as a man.

I did not trust any woman, and I viewed women as nothing. My view of my mother had me so twisted, I tried every woman to her, and that was not fair. Men, I am begging to seek help and get answers from your mother or father. You need to pursue your own understanding and not what others have to tell you about your parent. I cannot tell you; they will answer or hold a conversation about said topics.

All I am saying is seek closure, so you can live your life without chains. This is your redemption story, and it is a part of your life story. You need this freedom for yourself, your mate, your kids, and anyone else in your life.

We cannot allow the fear of the truth to push us away from the facts. I must be honest with you; your mother or father probably lied on the other one for years. And you might have to take a step back and regroup yourself, but you will know the truth about your life. Once you gathered the correct information, that will move you towards redeeming your life.

This will be a challenging task to confront your mother or father but is your life worth still suffering because you want to save their ego. Men, you know, just like I knew, I was damaging my kids and women. We are the leaders, and we cannot be scared to get answers. This is your redemption story, and this will be the cycle.

So, as I speak today, my mother and I have a great relationship, we talk often, and I have discovered we are similar in so many ways. My love for my mother is deep; I love her, I respect her, I admire her, I would not ask God for a different mother, and I seek out her for knowledge and insight on various issues.

So, our redemption story is huge for my life and my future endeavors. I understand clearly who I am now. My mother is solid as a rock and has helped me in so many ways. Most of all, I learned to respect women and hold them in high regard. Our women are the Queens; we must protect, honor, provide for and lead in the right direction. I will never treat women the same again, because of the hurt I was carrying around.

Furthermore, I have other issues that destroyed me for years and I had to seek treatment. I was molested when I was very young and that messed me up. I was a kid battling within my young mind on this topic. I did not get any counseling. I was basically left alone with nightmares and confusion on what gender I should be dealing with. After doing my own research and watching others, and at that point, I figured it out. And that was not good for me.

Fellows, let us be real and stop being ashamed for what a coward did to you. It is on that adult person who took advantage of you, not you. I repeat a child sex-offender is the problem, not you, my brother. I sincerely encourage you to seek help as soon as possible. I encourage you to speak with someone in your life. I was 25 years old when I told my best friend Sleepy Robinson. I cannot recall how we got on the topic or if I just had to get off my chest. But I was comfortable telling him because I knew he would not use it against me nor spread it like a wildfire.

Men, you will have to be careful about who you share this information with as well. I know some people who live to use your pain as a crutch for them to attack you at any moment. And that is one of the chances you take because everyone isn't real and doesn't have your best interest at heart. You cannot be consumed with soulless people. I hope you will not allow your fear to cancel your appointment with a counselor.

I will get into the damage that the event created for my life and how I disrespected myself and so many women after I went through this mental battle within my own mind. And I got back to my original knowledge men and women are the way it supposes to be. Now, some people decide the same-sex relationships are for them that is fine. I just love women, and until a few years ago, I wanted every woman possible.

My mind was so sick, I thought every woman owed me some sort of sexual encounter. I can remember I started watching porn at a young age, and I can recall it staying on my mind. It did not matter where I was; sex was always on my mind, and I did not care where I had it. We can be in the car, park, my job, restaurant bathrooms, I or whatever she would say okay.

I went to my first therapy sessions about this sex problem at 17 years old. That was a waste of my dad's money, and I cannot remember one word he said after I left the building. I started having sex at 13 years old and by the time I was 16, I was having sex no less than 3 times a day. In my sick mind, I had to prove to myself that I was not gay nor had any feelings for boys.

I went so many years on this track of self-destruction and with no end in sight. I had no respect for myself and did not love myself. So, men, let us stop thinking because we are running through different women, we the man around town.

No, we are stupid, selfish, reckless, and destroying our temples daily. We have allowed society to classify women as a whore or whatever demeaning adjective we use, but what are you?

At the age of 37, I took myself to get help, and I went through a 40-day program in Frisco, Texas. I had to redeem myself. My out-of-control sexual desires had ruined my family. I lost everyone around me. My attitude and treatment towards my family were horrible. My whole life was driven by sex, and I had to get my life back in order. This program gave me the tools to guide me to a new life, self-respect, love and so much more for my life.

I got the tools; I needed to avoid my triggers and move differently in life. I will not go deeper into the situations out of respect for my family. I was wrong and lowdown for my actions. I deal with these desires daily, but I would not ever sell myself out like that again.

I made it my obligation to apologize for the hurt I caused my family. I will continue to redeem myself but speaking out to help others, plus show the people who believe in me. I will also have an open dialogue with my Queen about things and share my body with her and only her. I hope she is ready.

But, seriously, my guys, a terrible situation like I am discussing with you, can and will be a part of you losing everything. The best way to redemption in this situation is to seek counseling, heaving praying and just be open with yourself. Redemption falls on the truth at the end of the day. You will not be able to start your journey of redemption until you drop on your knees, pray, and open yourself up for different topics. You must be secure within yourself to be a driving force in your life. And once you have a true self-elevation with yourself, you on the way to heights you never imagined.

I finally became comfortable with myself. I no longer must be someone else to be comfortable around other people. I do not have to lie and pick away at other people's lives to feel great about myself. A lot of humans are totally for cutting your light so they can shine for a second, minute, hour, day, months, and some for years. But I do not want you to be fooled by their actions.

The accurate measure of a person is a man or woman who can stand in a mess and come out of it. A genuine person can speak on their issues and help others grow, but most people in your life will never grow up and let people see who they truly are.

I was tired of giving people less than real, so I decided it was my openness about my life. I could regain control of my life and help millions of people thrive in their life. I start at home and work outward, and I will ask you to do the same. Be honest and everything else will be just fine in life.

Redemption is excellent and a lot of people will question you and continue to hold you to your past. Please, I need you to understand, they have the problem now, not you. I repeat that person who is trying their hardest to hold you down. They are terrified of you discovering you are great and more powerful than they will ever be in life.

YOU, THE WINNER, AND THEY ARE STILL LOST. THEY ARE SURROUNDED BY DEPENDENT PEOPLE AND THESE PEOPLE MAKE THEM FEEL SECURE IN THEIR LIFE. ALSO, TAKE A MOMENT AND LOOK AT THEIR CIRCLE. NO ONE ELSE IS A BOSS. ARE YOU READY TO START YOUR REDEMPTION START?

You have someone that poured into you, so do not let their hard work go in vain. You must stand up and pour into other people. That is why I am on my redemption tour. I will be this powerful public speaker and life coach until God calls me home.

I am unbreakable, unshakable, and unapologetic real plus bold. You do not know you in the presence of the greatest. I will outwork you and my grind is different than yours. It is my job to make Robinson's legacy last until the year 3020.

And in addition to what you learn and teach…. teach and motivate to have crazy FAITH!!!!!!!! a little education with some immense, wild faith…. unstoppable

Wow grocery this been a wild ride; I wrote my first book, yes you heard me, I wrote my first book, REDEMPTION. Me the country boy from Mississippi, Starkvegas, as we call it. The kid who did not like to read nor write. A KID WHO WAS LOST FOR 30 PLUS YEARS. A KID WHO HAS ALL THE TALENT IN THE WORLD BUT ALLOWED DIFFERENT DECISIONS TO MAP OUT HIS LIFE.

Redemption: The Next Phase…

A MAN WHO NEVER TURNED THAT CORNER TO BECOME A GROWN MAN UNTIL LATER IN LIFE. A KID WHO ONLY WANTED LOYALTY AND REALNESS FROM OTHERS. A KID WHO WANTED TO FILL HOLES WITH LOVE, BUT ONLY WAS CROSSED AND FOCUSED ON THE DOUBLE CROSS. A MAN, WHO MADE TONS OF MONEY FOR ME AND OTHERS, BUT JACKED IT OFF. I AM THE PICTURE OF REDEMPTION. I LOST IT ALL, FAMILY, FRIENDS, LOVE ONES, AND ETC

The small place where stars are born and raised. I am talking about Antuan Edwards the first-ever NFL 1st round draft pick. I am talking about the home of Frank Nicholas, the first African American police chief. I am talking about the birthplace of Clifton Bishop, the first-ever street general turned Charter Boat company owner. I am talking about Travis Outlaw, the first-ever high school to NBA first-round draft pick. I am talking about Jerry Rice, the most excellent wide receiver in NFL history. I am speaking about Cool Papa Bell.

The next one up is me: Bert Robinson, the first public speaker and life coach out of Starkville, Mississippi. I was built for this.

I will continue to bring you the knowledge and help you open your mind, heart, body, and soul to changes—this the beginning of my new life.

My REDEMPTION. I would like to personally thank you for taking your hard-earned money and time reading my book.
Much Love and Respect.

But before I get out of here. I must thank some people, and if I forgot to mention you, please charge it to my head, not the heart.

My Grandfather Burton L. Robinson, My Grandmother Nancy G. Robinson, My beautiful mom Mildred Bailey, and Warrior Dad, "Boss Hog" William B. Robinson, Sr. William "Sleepy" Robinson, Marcus Watt, Troy Robinson, Steve "Hammer" Robinson, Mike Robinson, Don Brooks, Karen Robinson, Marcus Grant, Fredrick "bad made-up" Barnes & Family, Tammy Darden, Toni Guydon, Terry Self, Uncle Jessie Bell, Blair Bell & Family, Aunt Helen Odom, Aunt Linda Robinson, BIG D Young & Family, Demarcus Bailey, Johnnie Bailey, Pamela Elliott, Big Bro B, Milton Smith & Family, Jeff Akins & Family, Kenyon Self & Family, Kalie Minor & Family, Reggie Williams, Kimble Hill, Von Gray, Calvin Young, Abdural Lee, Tiffany Pendelton, Jerold Poe, Lateff Travis, Robert Young, Bobby Boyd, Big Sis Angie Grant, Doug Bell & Family, My brother from another Bobby Williams, Clifton Bishop, Antuan Edwards, Antwin Edwards, Carlos Clark, Dawn Mann & Family, Mr. & Mrs. Williams, DR. G Lamont, MY CHI-TOWN PARTNERS, Marcus Brooks, Denise Collier, Damita Harper, Kimberly Jones, and last be never last Daelyn

Patton, Deyszjah Robinson, Sha'king Allah, Elizabeth Robinson, Jada Dockery, Shamone Barnes and William Robinson, III.

God will use your deepest and darkest moments to launch you to your greatest calling. When you are going through those periods in your life. Please take that time to grow and plan out your life. My most significant accomplishments were developed in the pandemic.

These moments of commitment come with superpower forces that are embedded in your character: an adamantine, unbreakable, and unshakable conviction that what you are doing is unequivocally right.

SO, WHAT IS YOUR REDEMPTION STORY?

If you around success, you breathe success,

BERT ROBINSON

Thanks, and Recognition to...

Frank "Historian" Nicholas

First of all, thank you, I can express how much, I appreciate you and all you have done for me and so many people in this world. I'm proud to have some of the same bloodline running through my body. Regardless of what timeframe, we have crossed path, you showed much respect and love. The concerned about me and my family when I called for help will never be forgotten. The countless of encouragement you given me during my journey of change and redemption has been impactful for my life. As you continue to give your life and service to everyone else, I would like for you to understand that without outstanding men as yourself. This world wouldn't be as great. Thank you for writing the foreword for the book Redemption and most of all, I thank God for you daily.

Much love and respect,

Bert.

How one adult conversation can change the entire understanding and views on your upbringing? For so many years, I never knew or understood, why I left my mom's house to live with my grandmother? I had so much anger, hurt, and anguish for no reason. But, this setting, this conversation on and off camera answered everything I been wondering for 35 years. My people a lot of damaged or no relationships happens because parties involved are fearful of the truth or never have a simple conversation. Open your heart, mind, body, and soul to the truth and redefine your life.

Redemption: The Next Phase…

My grandmother Nancy G Robinson

My Dad William B. Robinson Sr.

My Brothers

Family

Queen Ms. Bishop

Redemption: The Next Phase…

My Children

To my kids, I APOLOGIZE.

My journey started back in 1998, I became a father, I had no idea, what I was doing. I was just a lost child myself. For the last 22 years, I been on different rides in life. I been dealing with my own problems with abandonment, confusion, trust issues, addiction, and doing somethings that I knew wasn't right.

I continually pray for your life on a daily basis and ask God to keep you'll covered in His Blood. As you walk your own individual paths in life, you will start to understand how life can take you for a ride. Therefore, I hope my mishaps will give you a picture of what not to do in life, but at the same time, you will understand about Grace and Mercy. I could go on for years explaining life, but this book has given you insight into my life experiences and how to overcome different challenges.

The world is yours and make sure you impact on other's lives.

Love,

Pops

Children continued…

Bert Robinson

Sha'King Allah

Jason Minor

Redemption: The Next Phase…

Redemption: The Next Phase…

Bert Robinson

Blair Bell

As I think back, we are one of the same people. I can recall when you and Uncle Jessie pulled up in the Toyota and you sat in the car seat just looking. You were 18 months old, and I was the 13-year-old big brother.

My love, care, and concern for you grew each day. Throughout the years, I have made many mistakes in showing you; how a kid and men show roll? But the Power of God. My lil bro, I'm so proud of the man, father, and soon to be husband, you have become. I can't wait to see more. Yes, we had some tribulations, and you know me, to walk with me those are bound to happen. I will always be right next to you. I will always be down for you, and I will always be ready to ride with you.

Bert & Jessie still rolling together.

BB4L

Love & Loyalty,

Big Bro Pooh

Sleepy

You already know what it is.

A bond that started between a father and a father-in-law was the foundation that was laid for us. Then a sister and her best friend continue building on that foundation. Those relationships and solid relationships lead to the day, I was over your apartment with my sister getting help with some homework. I had no idea what relationship were being built between you and my father, but I'm so thankful for those moments.

You taught me about the 3 F's (Family, Faith, and Finances). You showed me life, you understood life, you had already experienced the downs, I would endure in life. So, you gave me Free game, inspiration and so much more.

When everyone turned their back on my father, but you were there. The rides to Ackerman every Tuesday for frog legs before he died.

This one is a dedication to you.

WBR4L

LOYALTY, LOVE, AND RESPECT,

Pooh

Bert Robinson

Best Friends, My Girls

Angie, I always adored you and I always wanted to be with you. A brother couldn't ask for a more real sister. You know the journey, so I hope, I made you proud and smile. I thank God for your life, encouraging words, love, honesty, and so much more.

Karen, you opened up your house when I was living in my car, or a roach infested hotel. After three smiles, jokes, and disappointing actions, you were always down for me. I still have that little education and crazy Faith that will take me to the top.

My girls, I love you'll for life,

Pooh

Bert Robinson

www.ingramcontent.com/pod-product-compliance
Lightning Source LLC
Chambersburg PA
CBHW052109110526
44592CB00013B/1545